MW01256029

The Rise and Fall of the Sugar King

A History of Williamsburg, Brooklyn 1844-1909

Geoffrey Cobb

NB | NORTH BROOKLYN
NH | NEIGHBORHOOD HISTORY

Copyright ©2017 by Geoffrey Cobb. All rights reserved.

This book may not be reproduced, in whole or in part, in any form (beyond that copying permitted by Sections 107 and 108 of the U.S. Copyright Law and except by reviewers of the public press), without written permission from the publishers.

Geoffrey Cobb is the sole author of *The Rise and Fall of the Sugar King: A History of Williamsburg, Brooklyn 1844-1909.*

ISBN-10: 197841546X

ISBN-13: 978-1978415461

Printed in the United States of America.

Contents

Introduction..iii

Chapter One: Rising Steeples..1

Chapter Two: An Unwelcomed Church...12

Chapter Three: to the Church!..28

Chapter Four: October 18, 1859, A Martyr Predicts Civil

War...37

Chapter Five: The Death of the Philantropist - May 21,

1860..50

Chapter Six: Another Sugar Empire Rises....................................58

Chapter Seven: Steam and Sugar.......................................67

Chapter Eight: Sugar Refining Arrives in Williamsburg........76

Chapter Nine: Early Civil War Years................................85

Chapter Ten: July, 1863...99

Contents

Chapter Eleven: The War Finally Ends..........................111

Chapter Twelve: Apprenticeships..............................119

Chapter Thirteen: Love and Wars - 1867.....................130

Chapter Fourteen: Collections - 1876........................142

Chapter Fifteen: A Phoenix Rises from the Ashes of Despair -

January 8, 1882..179

Chapter Sixteen: Strikes - 1886..............................196

Chapter Seventeen: Bonds of Trust?..........................213

Chapter Eighteen: Gladiators.................................228

Chapter Nineteen: Trustworthy Politicians?..................248

Chapter Twenty: The Cynical State Senator Takes

Control...270

Chapter Twenty-One: Ill Gotten Gains........................287

Chapter Twenty-Two: Deaths..................................299

Chapter Twenty-Three: Hubris and The Scales of

Justice...308

Epilogue: 326

Introduction

The history of Williamsburg is so intertwined with the production of sugar that local history cannot be separated from the rise of the American sugar industry. About twenty years ago, I began to research Williamsburg's past, discovering its fascinating industrial history. The research was complicated because, unlike other areas of Brooklyn, there is no single volume that adequately recounts its early history. Williamsburg principally developed its urban industrial character because of the sugar industry, and for decades Williamsburg was the largest area for sugar refining on the planet, with seven sugar refineries lining the East River waterfront. Because of the massive local sugar industry, and the thousands of workers who labored for it, Williamsburg became at one time the most densely populated area in the country. The thousands of Polish immigrants who settled locally first came to toil in the unbearable heat of the refineries. The story of Williamsburg's sugar industry, as well as the neighborhood's history, however, is largely an untold story, but one that demands telling.

This book recounts the history of Williamsburg, Brooklyn's critical years of formation from 1845 to 1909. They witnessed the birth and settlement of the town of Williamsburg. They also saw nativist conflict between American-born citizens and newly arrived immigrants, and the Civil War with its draft riots, but most importantly, the book describes the industrial revolution in Williamsburg. During this period the area was transformed from an isolated, bucolic village into one of the most heavily industrialized urban areas in the world. These years in Williamsburg witnessed huge demographic changes, along with the forging of a massive working class who often toiled in dangerous, inhuman conditions for subsistence wages, while living in hundreds of overcrowded, unhealthy, airless tenements.

All of the characters and the events in the book are real. The book tells the stories of different authentic historical characters who lived through this era, including champion boxers, an African American abolitionist, a Catholic priest, a Civil War veteran turned police captain and a barrel maker turned corrupt politician. At times, I have used my imagination to describe possible thoughts or feelings that these persons may have felt to enhance their stories, yet everything the book describes is based on authentic historical research.

The Rise and Fall of the Sugar King- A History of Williamsburg Brooklyn principally tells the story of the area's refining barons, the Havemeyer clan, who are unquestionably the most influential family in Williamsburg history, but their true story has remained largely untold. The Havemeyers created one of the first, and most powerful, American corporate trusts, forming an illegal virtual monopoly that was the sixth-largest industrial corporation in the United States. The Havemeyers became fabulously wealthy thanks to the trust, but the Williamsburger workers who toiled, and sometimes even died, creating this vast wealth did not share much of it.

The book's central character is the most important member of that clan, a complicated character, and one of the richest Americans who ever lived: Henry O. Havemeyer, the imperious, multimillionaire father of the Sugar Trust, but also the source for the largest and most important donation ever to the Metropolitan Museum of Art. The donation of over a thousand pieces of priceless art Henry Havemeyer and his wife Lousine collected made the museum into one of the world's great art collections. This collection was bought with the profits made from Williamsburg sugar. Henry's grandson, Harry Havemeyer, wrote the sole biography of the sugar baron, titled: *Henry O. Havemeyer: The Most Independent Mind*, but it is in many ways a hagiography, praising him, while omitting the dark side, and criminal acts, of the "Sugar King."

The Havemeyer's rise to domination of the sugar industry casts a dark and sinister shadow over local history. The Williamsburg story is, to a great extent, also the story of American capitalism, and one of its most criminal chapters was written locally. A study of neighborhood history reveals Havemeyer's creation of vast wealth, power, greed and corruption. It is a crime story, but also the personal story of Henry O. Havemeyer's hubris, and his belief that his wealth and power had raised him above the law. Havemeyer's story is a tragic tale because the revelations of his crimes led him to an early grave. This book tells the story of how the Havemeyers created an international sugar empire that also shaped Williamsburg. It is most importantly the story of the tens of thousands of anonymous people, who toiled, suffered and even died building the great empire of the sugar king.

This book goes beyond mere local history. Sugar

refining in Williamsburg had a number of massive influences that not only affected Washington and the rest of the country, but were also felt far beyond America's borders, influencing not just American foreign policy, but also other countries' historical development. Some have called the Spanish-American War of 1898 "Havemeyer's War" because he promoted it as a means of wresting control of the sugar crop away from Spain. Willliamsburg refined massive amounts of Cuban sugar, transforming Cuba into an economic dependency of the United States, engendering a deep resentment that later helped to bring Fidel Castro to power.

Sometimes local history has little in common with broader American historical themes, but not in Williamsburg, where local history mirrors American history. Williamsburg history is in many respects a microcosm of American history. Many of the great issues of American history, immigration, the Civil War, Industrialization and labor history played out in the neighborhood. In fact, the crimes that were happening locally were of such magnitude that the president of the United States, Theodore Roosevelt, took a personal interest in them, and made sure that the culprits were prosecuted. These crimes were reported across the nation in dozens of American newspapers, and

Roosevelt's prosecution of Havemeyer's American Sugar Refining Company gained him a reputation as a "trust buster."

There is urgency to recording and saving Williamsburg's industrial past. The sugar industry, as well as many other industries, died leaving many abandoned plants in its wake. The abandoned factories at first became home to artists and other creative people, but soon Williamsburg's old factories became targets of developers, who realized that the factories could be torn down and replaced with luxury condos. Today the area is rapidly gentrifying, and sleek new condo towers are replacing historic factories, obliterating the area's important industrial landmarks. The Domino refinery itself will be transformed into a giant residential space, annihilating most of its industrial past. Williamsburg has a unique and fascinating industrial history. Hopefully, this book will help to preserve that past, accurately portraying the dramatic transformations the area witnessed.

Chapter One:
Rising Steeples

In the 1840s, Williamsburg echoed with the sounds of construction. A din of pounding hammers, and of boards being sawed, drowned out the normal sounds of town life. Carpenters, perched high above the ground on precarious scaffolds, were nailing planks into place on the steeples on the still-unpainted churches rising all around the town like mushrooms after a shower. The new steeples were rapidly forming a skyline, creating the town's first prominent landmarks, visible for miles from the flat surrounding farmland. Every resident seemed to be constantly looking up, gazing in awe at the new, lofty steeples arising before their eyes. Williamsburg was on a building binge, and these were not the only buildings going up, but for the devout residents, the most important structures taking shape were the many churches.

Until recently, there had only been one house of

worship in Williamsburg, the Dutch Reformed Church on the corner of Bedford and South Second, which was not yet two decades old, but had been the site of a place of worship since the seventeenth century. The original building, constructed on a bluff that also vanished, was so ancient that it had been both church and fort, not only serving as a house of prayer, but also as a sanctuary from Indian attacks. In 1828, men who had recently turned farmland into town lots constructed the new church themselves, building it with hand-hewn boards and homemade nails on what would later be called Bedford Avenue, but was then merely a rough country lane where pigs and other livestock roamed freely. The road proved treacherous for rider and horse with boulders, tree stumps, huge potholes and ubiquitous mud posing danger.

Not long ago, Protestants who did not belong to the Dutch Reformed faith were so few in number that they had to gather and pray in a non-denominational service at the Dutch Reformed church. In those days, there were not enough members of any sect to form their own church, but that changed quickly in the 1840s. Protestants of different denominations were arriving, each sect intent on building its own house of worship. The Congregationalists were constructing a New England-style meeting house at South Third

Street and Hewes Street in 1844. The Episcopalians were also building a church on South Second Street. The Baptists, who had earlier constructed a simple wood frame church on Driggs Avenue and South First Street, were building a more elegant Gothic structure with two graceful spires rising high above the town on South Fifth Street to house their surging congregation. Not to be outdone, the Methodists had also built a Gothic church on the corner of Grand Street and Manhattan Avenues in 1845. Their congregation also soon outgrew the old church, and they added another church on North Fourth Street between Berry and Bedford Avenues. The First Universalist Church & Society, in 1847 erected a brick building on the southwest corner of South Third Street & Bedford Avenue. The Presbyterians, the largest Protestant group, built an elegant, but austere house of worship on South Second Street and Roebling Streets in 1842. They soon built a second Presbyterian church on South Fourth Street, and finally they built a brick church on South Third Street.

Devout Williamsburgers must have felt in the 1840s that their prayers had finally been answered because the town had grown into a thriving commercial center. None could deny that it had become a truly prosperous town, and in their eyes, the Lord had been merciful lately, showering them with economic blessings. Steeples were not just soaring upwards; the economy was skyrocketing as well. Williamsburg had the good fortune to be situated just a mile and a half from Wall Street, right across the river from booming Manhattan, which had been transformed into the dominant industrial and financial city in the country by the 1825 opening of the Erie Canal. Williamsburg was attracting industry away from Manhattan, and by the late 1840s, the town had nine rope works, two shipyards, two tanneries, a pair of distilleries, a hat factory, a carpet mill and Peter Cooper's glue factory, the largest glue works in the country.

The town's growth seemed nothing short of miraculous to the few hundred people who had lived there before it became an independent village in 1827. In that year, a grid plan for the streets was laid out similar to the one Manhattan had adopted two years previously. For many years, though, the area had remained undeveloped, lagging far behind other areas of Long Island, due to many natural disadvantages preventing settlement. Farming the land was difficult because it was covered with thick bushes that were hard to chop out. The bushes, known by the Dutch as cripplebush, also gave an early name to the area. A scarcity of fresh inland water also prevented agriculture from flourishing, further retarding growth.

The greatest factor slowing the settlement of the area though was fear of disease. Constant tidal flooding from the East River left pools of stagnant water that were perfect breeding grounds for malarial mosquitos. Swamps were also an early Williamsburg feature, adding another home for disease-carrying insects. In 1790, and again in 1803, there were outbreaks of yellow fever that claimed lives. In 1847, the town was ravaged by an outbreak of ship's fever. The following year, cholera took the lives of 1,642 people. In fear of a repetition of such outbreaks, locals imported the famous ailanthus tree from China in the 1840s; a tree that flourished in the swampy, low-lying areas of Williamsburg. The tree became popular because of its supposed power to dispel the diseases arising from swamp vapors. The ailanthus tree later became the defining symbol of Williamsburg in Betty Smith's iconic novel *A Tree Grows in Brooklyn*.

Some men had grown rich from the booming economy, but many of these wealthy residents still felt a strong civic duty, none more than the reclusive Noah Waterbury, who was called "the Father of Williamsburg." A generation previously, when there were only a few hundred people in the town he had started a distillery, which had prospered, making Waterbury a very wealthy man. His mansion at the foot of South Fifth Street was huge and graceful; however, it was not only Waterbury's palatial home, but also his sleek racing yacht anchored in the East River, the regatta winning ship *Julia*, that made people envy him. When Williamsburg became a village in 1827, it seemed natural to elect Waterbury as its first leader, despite his reclusiveness.

Providence had also showered the area with both great abundance and natural beauty. The East River not only boasted a beautiful shore with sand that rivaled any Long Island beach, but the waters also teemed with delicacies like porgies, eels, crabs, clams and oysters. Where the river met Bushwick Creek, there was an area of great natural beauty featuring a shady grove of willow trees and beds of wild flowers.

God, however, had not always been kind to the area. In the late 1840s, memories of the panic of 1837, and the deep depression that followed it, still haunted Williamsburgers. In the first half of the 1830s, Williamsburg real estate seemed like the perfect investment. Lithographed property maps set forth in glowing terms the unrivaled opportunities to make easy money. Developers in the 1830s built fourteen large, elegant, model homes at the intersection of Grand

Street and Union Avenue to encourage Manhattan investors to buy vacant lots, and the town started to grow rapidly. An orgy of speculation ensued, fueled by rich Manhattan merchants, nine-tenths of whom were buying on the margin and hoping to flip the lots quickly. Some investors were so certain that Williamsburg would develop into an exclusive suburb of Manhattan that they bought up hundreds of lots, sight unseen, on any given day. A huge bubble quickly formed. The value of real estate reached absurd proportions as investors looked to buy and sell at a profit. Prices soared so high that they reached a level in 1836 that they still would not reach again until sixteen years later in 1852.

The prospect of vast real estate fortunes stimulated greed and fraud. Some Williamsburgers decided fraudulently to cash in on the real estate frenzy, conniving with equally corrupt town officials to deprive Manhattan investors of their lots by vastly overvaluing their properties, creating huge tax liabilities the investors could not meet. 10,000 lots were sold in Williamsburg for nonpayment of taxes. When the properties were foreclosed, these scheming locals bought the lots at fire sale prices with borrowed money. Their scheme blew up in their faces when the Panic of 1837 hit, and credit completely dried up. A number of houses were left half built. The schemers, and other investors, suffered foreclosure, and business in the town soon ground to a halt. The only local bank failed, and even the steam ferry went out of business. The hard times did not abate until 1842, when prosperity slowly returned.

The real estate crash of 1837, though, was not the first time in Williamsburg history when developers went bankrupt. In 1792, the first local developer, Manhattan merchant Richard Woodhull, bought up and tried to develop 15 acres of farmland around North Second Street, having it surveyed into streets and lots by Jonathon Williams, Benjamin Franklin's grandson. Woodhull named the planned community Williamsburg in the surveyor's honor.

Woodhull also began a ferry to Manhattan, but Williamsburg was isolated, and the ferry journey proved both long and perilous. Ferries often overturned for a number of reasons, including tricky gusts of wind, summer squalls, drifting ice and even the sudden movement of the horses powering the ferry. Ferry service was also often suspended after dark because it was deemed too dangerous. The lack of a road along the shore also made Woodhull's ferry hard to reach. Not surprisingly, few people were attracted to his new development.

Woodhull soon had competition from another developer who bought land just to the south of Woodhull's parcel of land, also dreaming of creating a new fashionable community. In 1804, Thomas Morrell from Newtown, in what is now Queens, petitioned the state and started a rival ferry, certain that it would attract settlers from Manhattan. He purchased twenty-eight acres from Folkert Titus, a local farmer, whose land extended from North Second Street to South First Street along the river, and Morrell, like Woodhull, had the land surveyed and divided into lots. He cut a road through the middle of the old farm, which he called Grand Street, and called the site of the ferry Morrell Point. A stone wall at the southern edge of his property formed the boundary between Williamsburg and Brooklyn, hence it acquired the name Division Street. Morrell succeeded in driving Woodhull into bankruptcy in 1811, and by 1814, he owned all the land between Wallabout Bay and Bushwick Inlet, but the same factors that prevented Woodhull from successfully developing a suburb also prevented Morrell from achieving his vision of creating a thriving community. One business venture of Morrell's, though, did succeed. The old Titus farmhouse became the Fountain Inn, which was located on North Second Street. It became the most popular local tavern, and the center of local life, until it burned down in 1840.

There were many reasons for Williamsburgers in the 1840s to be optimistic about the future, but the locals also had many reasons to worry. When the economy rebounded, speculators had gained the upper hand over those who wanted to build a middle-class community of homeowners. Rich men had built beautiful homes next to the Woodbury mansion. These elegant colonnaded structures resembled George Washington's Mount Vernon, and commanded views of Governor's Island, but the rich who owned these homes were driven out of the area because speculators built tawdry row houses that repulsed the rich. The speculators also sold waterfront lots to industrialists who built factories and warehouses along the shoreline, ruining the chance of creating an elegant suburb and forever changing Williamsburg's character.

The speculators also erected flimsy cottages on the lots they owned that could be rented out for a hundred dollars a year, while earning a twelve-percent annual return on the investment. These cottages attracted the indigent, and thousands of poor people now began to populate the area. Residents soon grew apprehensive about a dangerous group of impoverished foreigners who were arriving locally in great numbers, attracted by the cheap rents the cottages offered. These people, in the eyes of many locals, posed a threat to the community and its values. These people's unwelcome church was also rising in the very heart of the town. While the construction of the Protestant churches filled most of the townspeople with a conviction that God was playing a role in the town's growth and prosperity, the construction of this new church scared many people, for its congregants were unwanted refugees. Their presence in such large numbers was to many a dark cloud on the horizon. Many residents even wanted to drive these dangerous unwelcome foreigners out of Williamsburg. Religious conflict loomed.

Chapter Two:
An Unwelcomed Church

The winter of 1847-1848 was an unusually mild one, allowing builders to work on winter days when during most other winters no building took place. The talk of Williamsburg that winter was the new Gothic church arising at Wythe Avenue and South Second Street. Everyone reluctantly agreed that the new church under construction was more graceful than any other house of worship in the town, yet few were happy to see it built, or its congregants settle in their town. The Church of Saints Peter and Paul was an Irish Catholic church, an unwelcome presence for many in staunchly anti-Catholic Williamsburg.

Another group of Catholics had settled in the area previously, but they were German Catholics who did not elicit the same visceral, negative reactions that the Irish did. Hundreds of German-speaking Catholics had followed an Austrian priest, Father Johann Raffeiner, who came to Williamsburg in the summer of 1841 to start the first German Catholic church in Brooklyn. Using mostly his own money, he bought an isolated piece of the Abraham Meserole farm on Montrose Avenue and constructed a simple wood-frame church. Seven years later, the church had grown to fifteen hundred parishioners. The Germans were, by and large, well-educated, diligent, skilled artisans, capable of making a good living, so they were tolerated, even if most Williamsburg natives mistrusted their religion. Communication difficulties with English-speaking Williamsburgers led the area to misnamed "Dutch Town."

The new church was rising at a time of strong anti-Catholic feeling in America. Many saw the construction of Saints Peter and Paul in a darker light than the building of the German church. The construction of this Irish church was for them a provocation. They said that building such a grand Catholic edifice in the very heart of the town had some dark significance, believing that the church here was part of a sinister, secret plan by the Pope to take over America. They worried that the church would attract even more impoverished aliens into their midst, who would undermine the Yankee virtue of hard work that had built Williamsburg. They thought the Irish primitive, dangerous and incapable of change. They also wondered how a group as poor as the Irish could build such an expensive church, suggesting sinister sources of its funding.

Locals also complained about the devious way the church had acquired the lot on which the church was rising. The Catholic priest, realizing residents would balk at selling the land for a Catholic church, had not bought the land himself, but instead acquired it surreptitiously through a parishioner who never told the owners his true intentions for the property. The Catholic priest sat on the lot for eighteen months, and then one day he suddenly announced that the plans for church's construction, right in the heart of the town, much to the consternation to the towns many bigots.

Even if they were unhappy about its construction, Williamsburgers, all the same, had a lurid fascination with the beautiful structure rising on South Second Street that winter. Its graceful façade was so different than the austere Protestant churches they knew that many locals walked out of their way each day just to gawk at the church. Nothing on its scale had ever been built before in the area, and it soon became one of the most popular subjects of town gossip. Although they resented its construction, they still marveled at its elegance and beauty, secretly wondering how such a primitive people could build such a beautiful church. The new church had a gabled roof with a tall, thin elegant tower, topped by the tallest steeple in the town. The tower was eighteen feet at its base with a height of seventy feet, and four pinnacles rising off the tower, marking its edges. The steeple reached a height of a hundred and fifty feet off the ground. The church had large, gracefully arched widows in the façade and a series of buttresses along its sides, under which rose seven high-arched Gothic stained glass windows. The church's exterior was being finished in a graceful stucco that resembled brownstone.

The grand design of the church was the idea of an ambitious Irish immigrant, Father Sylvester Malone, an energetic twenty-six-year-old priest who had been assigned to the area just three years previously. A visionary, Malone planned to make a statement in stone, proclaiming the glory of his faith and the huge presence of his people in the community. The new church was bold and in total contrast to St. Mary's church, which it was replacing. St. Mary's was a modest, unobtrusive wood- frame building, which seemed almost to cower at the outskirts of the town at North Eighth Street. Malone not only inherited this small wooden church, but also a two thousand dollar debt, preventing him from building a new church. He exhorted his rapidly growing congregation to liquidate the debt so that he could build a newer church, large enough to house his rapidly increasing flock. His congregation responded to his appeal, and soon he was free of the debt, ready to take on building a church of an entirely different character.

Malone needed a master builder, and he prayed that God would reveal one to him. Soon his prayers seemed to be answered in the person of a fellow Irishman named Patrick Keely, whom Malone anointed as the builder of his church. Keely had arrived in America five years previously in 1842, at the age of twenty-six. His father, who had built the elegant Saint Patrick College in his hometown, Thurles, County Tipperary, taught him the fundamentals of building, but Keely had not been prepared to build the elaborate Gothic structure Malone intended. A diffident, pious man, Keely at first complained that he was a mere carpenter, unworthy of Malone's faith that he could build such a grand church. As a Catholic in his native land, Keely had been forbidden to study architecture by the draconian Penal Laws, which relegated him and other Catholics to the lowest rungs of the Irish social hierarchy.

Malone, however, encouraged him to take on the project, saying that through prayer he would find the wherewithal to plan and build the church. A man of great faith, Malone believed in miracles, and he was certain that his young architect would not falter. Malone also reminded Keely of his duty to his people. The Potato Famine back home was driving tens of thousands of starving Irishmen to America, many of whom would end up here, desperately needing a church.

Finally, Keely reluctantly agreed. The two Irishmen worked out the plans for the church together, which they presented to Bishop John Hughes, who initially rejected them because of their exorbitant cost. However, Malone persisted, and finally Hughes relented, allowing the construction to proceed. Keely worked intensely directing the building of the church, but fearing failure, he prayed fervently each night that God would allow him to successfully build such a monumental building. When the congregations saw the grand plans for the church, they were awestruck, for they could not imagine that this great building would be their own church. A number of them were from the countryside in Ireland where they had only prayed in rude chapels. Inspired by the project, many of the parishioners even volunteered to help him build the church. The local Irish took pride in its construction, and it became a communal task, with many pitching in to build the beautiful house of worship.

Many of Malone's flock, though, remembered that their religion was regarded as satanic by many of their Protestant neighbors, and they knew the Irish were not welcome in Williamsburg. Some in the congregation expressed fears that the central location of the new church would foment violence. They even encouraged Malone to build the parish house behind the church to shield the priest from nativist attacks. The young priest, however, would not hear of such cowardice. Malone believed that the American sense of fair play would triumph, and that he and his congregation would be welcomed into the community—a belief many of his congregation regarded as naïve and dangerous.

By 1847, Malone had become a familiar, albeit unwelcome, face in Williamsburg. He had a broad face and kind, intelligent blue eyes, but the bigots never saw his face, just the Roman collar he wore. Sadly, to the bigots it did not matter that Malone loved America and would teach his flock to love it too. He had loved America and its promise of freedom and equality long before he had ever seen it. It was said of the Irish that the minute they set foot in New York they became American, and it was completely true of Malone, who became a passionate lover of his new country and its democratic institutions. Ironically, Malone loved America fervently, even if it did not love him or his people, and he was determined to defeat the bigotry he and his people were facing.

Malone never forgot that in his native land Catholics were persecuted for their faith, despite being a huge majority of the population. In1836, Malone's father passed away, and the fifteen-year-old boy must have realized that his future prospects in Ireland were limited. As for many of his generation, America seemed a land where a young Irishman could realize his potential. In 1838, his cousin, Father Andrew Byrne of St. James Church in Manhattan, went to Ireland to recruit young men for the priesthood. He met the seventeen-year-old Malone who impressed him with his piety, intelligence and capacity for organization. Byrne offered Malone the chance to come to America to study for the priesthood, and Malone gladly accepted the offer. He left the next year, arriving in Philadelphia in 1839.

Unlike many of his fellow Irishmen, Malone had no enmity towards Protestants and counted many as his friends, despite their being beneficiaries of the British rule in Ireland. He believed in the essential goodness of American Protestants, sure that over time they would come to accept his faith and his people. Unlike the vast majority of Catholic Irishman, Malone was fortunate enough to receive an education from the Protestant Carroll brothers, who ran a local academy where Protestant and Catholic children learned together, as equals without bigotry. Malone made friends with many Protestant classmates, and these friendships created a lifelong respect for all Christians, allowing Malone to develop a sincere respect for Protestants few other Catholic priests had.

Malone's love of America and Protestants would be put to the test immediately upon his arrival in Philadelphia. It was a time of intense anti-Catholicism there, the same bigotry with which he would soon become all too familiar in Williamsburg. He was warned about the hatred he would meet in America as a Catholic, but he was determined to be a model of Christian forbearance and to turn the other cheek. The large numbers of Irish Catholics arriving in the city of Brotherly Love had stirred up latent anti-Catholicism, and the response was an anti-immigrant ideology called nativism. America in general, and Philadelphia in particular, was bitterly opposed to Irish-Catholic immigration—especially to those, like Malone, who hoped to build a strong Catholic church on its shores. Nativists claimed that the Catholic religion was a threat to America's Protestant culture. Nativists and Evangelicals characterized Catholicism as an authoritative religion, incompatible with republicanism. Viewed as submissive and unquestioning followers, those of Catholic faith were seen as lacking the individuality and free thought required of democratic citizens. Moreover, the Catholic immigrant, whose allegiance was to a foreign ruler, was seen as disloyal to America.

In Philadelphia, Malone met a fellow Irishman whom he quickly grew to idolize, and who would become a lifelong friend, Archbishop "Dagger" John Hughes. Hughes and Malone would work to build the Catholic faith together in New York. Although he was a churchman, the fiery Hughes was more a Roman gladiator than a meek follower of Christianity. Born in 1797, in County Tyrone, Ireland, Hughes was the son of a poor farmer. As a Catholic in British-ruled Ireland, he was, truly a second-class citizen from the day he was baptized, barred from ever owning a house worth more than five pounds or holding a commission in the army or navy. Catholics could neither run schools nor give their children a Catholic education. Priests had to be licensed by the government, which allowed only a few in the country. Any Catholic son could seize his father's property by becoming a Protestant.

Hughes burned with righteous indignation at anti-Catholicism. When Hughes was fifteen his younger sister, Mary, died, an unforgettable event that crystallized for him the injustice of English domination. English law barred the local Catholic priest from entering the cemetery gates to preside at her burial; the best he could do was to scoop up a handful of dirt, bless it and hand it to Hughes to sprinkle on the grave.

From early on, Hughes said, he had dreamed of "a country in which no stigma of inferiority would be impressed on my brow, simply because I professed one creed or another." A brilliant, passionate orator, Hughes could defend his church and his people like no other figure in America, and his defense of the church and the Irish thrilled Malone and other Irish immigrants. Ordained a priest in 1826, Hughes' first assignment was one of the toughest: the diocese of Philadelphia, seething with anti-Catholicism. A large dimension of the Protestant Revival, beginning there in the late 1820s, included militant attacks against the Catholic Church. Hughes was outraged. He didn't want Catholics to be treated as second-class citizens in America as they had been in Ireland, and he thought it his duty to speak out forcefully against the prejudice. He began a letter-writing campaign to the newspapers, decrying what he saw as a tendency toward chauvinistic nationalism in his new country.

In 1829, for instance, outraged by an editorial

in a Protestant religious newspaper about "traitor-ous popery," he wrote a caustic letter to its editorial board of Protestant ministers, calling them "the cler-ical scum of the country." During the 1834 cholera epidemic in Philadelphia, which nativists blamed on Irish immigrants, Hughes worked tirelessly among the sick and dying, risking his life, while many Prot-estant ministers fled the city to escape infection. After the disease abated, Hughes wrote the *U.S. Gazette* that Protestant ministers were "remarkable for their pas-toral solicitude, so long as the flock is healthy, the pas-tures pleasant, and the fleece lubricant, abandoning their post when disease begins to spread dissolution in the fold." He highlighted in contrast the work of the Catholic Sisters of Charity, who had cared for cholera victims without regard for their own safety.

The following year, Hughes became a hero to American Catholics when a prominent and well-born Protestant clergyman from New York named John Breckenridge challenged him to a debate. The debate riveted both Protestants and Catholics. Breckenridge luridly conjured up the Catholic Church's Inquisition in Spain, tyranny in Italy and repression of liberty in France. Americans, he said, wanted no popery, no loss of individual liberty. Hughes countered by describ-ing Protestant tyranny over Catholic Ireland. He related what had happened at his sister's grave. "I am an American by choice, not by chance," he said. "I was born under the scourge of Protestant persecution, of which my fathers in common with our Catholic countrymen, have been the victim for ages. I know the value of that civil and religious liberty, which our happy government secures for all." Regardless of what had happened in Europe, he said, he was committed to American tolerance. Hughes won the debate in the eyes of American Catholics, and his defense of the Irish and the Catholic Church inspired Malone to fight against bigotry.

Bishop Hughes advised Malone to enter St. Joseph's Seminary in Jefferson County, New York, which he did. The following year the seminary moved to Rose Hill, on the campus of what would become Fordham University, where Malone completed his training for the priesthood. In the meantime, Hughes had been named Bishop of the New York Diocese. Needing a strong, levelheaded priest to build a church in the cauldron of Nativist sentiment that was Williamsburg, he named Malone to serve there in 1844, the year of his ordination.

Those early years of his priesthood were hard ones for Malone. The church lacked resources even to buy him a horse, and Malone had to visit his scattered congregation on foot. He often had to walk miles through snow and rain to tend to his flock who were spread out over great distances, but his greatest sufferings were not physical, but emotional. As a Catholic priest walking through nativist Williamsburg, Malone was the target of numerous anti-Catholic slurs, especially by volunteer fire department men who practically ran the area, and proved especially cruel in their taunting. Despite the daily heckling he received, Malone resolved never to respond in anger and proved himself a model of Christian forbearance. Years later, Malone recalled how he dealt with this abuse:

> I had my trials. They were long and they demanded patience on my part. Time and time again, my name was rudely called aloud in public by passing thoughtless boys and by young hangers-on of the old volunteer fire engine hose. I avoided being over severe in my language, or showing any anger, for I always reasoned with the one whom I thought was the aggressor and what was strange, I never found one to own up to the fact.

Malone had no illusions about the depth of nativist antipathy. He and his congregation had to be alarmed when they learned of two days of nativist riots that had targeted Irish Catholics in Philadelphia's Kensington section. The city's Bishop Kenrick appealed to his fellow Catholics to maintain the peace, and people hung flags from their windows and scrawled "Native American" on their doors in charcoal, hoping in vain to escape more violence. But the nativists descended on Kensington for a third day, burning down St. Michael's Church at Second and Jefferson and finishing off the seminary of the Sisters of Charity. The mob then torched St. Augustine's at Fourth Street and Vine as well as a nearby school. All told, fourteen more people died in the mayhem, fifty were injured, and hundreds lost their homes. Many Williamsburg Catholics feared the same kind of violence would repeat itself in Brooklyn, and they feared the church they were building would suffer the same fate.

Soon the church was completed, and people were in awe of what Keely had managed to create. Bishop Hughes dedicated the church itself on May 7, 1848. Almost the entire Catholic community in Williamsburg showed up, not only to celebrate the dedication of the church, but also to see their famous bishop. They cheered him wildly when he arrived locally, with everyone creening their necks to get a glimpse of their hero, the fiery bishop.

If the Catholics celebrated, then some of their

nativist neighbors fumed at the construction of the church, even going so far to consider its destruction as a defense of American values. Many local Catholics still harbored grave doubts, fearing a repeat of the Philadelphia riots. These fears of the destruction of their church would prove justified.

Chapter Three:
"to the Church!"

Throughout the late 1840s and into the early 1850s, as Manhattan emerged as the commercial capital of the United States, Williamsburg's economy also boomed. The population dramatically increased, but the seeds of conflict between the Nativists and Irish immigrants remained. An immigrant influx into Williamsburg occurred, increasing the potential for a repeat of the violence that had erupted in Philadelphia. Williamsburg was becoming far more prosperous, but the area was still a volatile powder keg, with many fearing that a single spark would ignite terrible violence.

By 1852, Williamsburg had grown so quickly that it outgrew its status as a town and received a charter as a city, being organized into three wards. The First Ward roughly coincided with the South Side, and the Second Ward with today's North Side, with Grand

Street marking the dividing line. The Third Ward was to the east of these areas, stretching from Union Avenue eastwards to Bushwick Avenue, which divided it from the town of Bushwick.

Much of the growth of Williamsburg's economy resulted from the relocation of Manhattan industry. Speculators, realizing they could profit by leasing lots to industry, forsook residential housing and leased to factory owners and heavy industries, quickly changing the waterfront into an industrial zone. Shipbuilding also moved quickly from Manhattan to Williamsburg's East River shore. Jabez Williams first moved his shipyard across the East River in 1845. Williams had been constructing vessels in New York since at least 1821, but realizing that land was much cheaper in Williamsburg, he relocated his shipyard. By the early 1850s, Thomas Stack, another Manhattan shipbuilder, followed him across the East River, setting up his yard along the water covering an area from North Fourth Street to North Sixth Street. A number of iron foundries, which often supplied shipbuilders, also opened in the area, as well as other kinds of industries, quickly making Williamsburg one of the most industrialized areas in America.

Thanks in large part to the booming economy, just two years after becoming a city, Williamsburg by 1854 had grown into the seventh-largest municipality in the nation, with an estimated population of 30,000 souls, but much of that growth was due to the expansion of the Catholic immigrant communities the Nativists detested. A quarter of the population Williamsburg population was now German, as Dutch Town grew to dominate the Third Ward, thanks in large part to frustrated German democrats who left after the 1848 revolution failed. The Irish population also continued to grow rapidly, with ships even sometimes illegally landing Irish immigrants directly on the Williamsburg shore, bypassing immigration controls at Castle Garden, enflaming nativist resentment. A third of the Williamsburg population soon became Irish, and half that third was foreign-born. An Irish area sprung up around Union Street called the Green, and thanks to the rapidly increasingly population, the Irish became more assertive locally, ready to physically confront their Nativist enemies.

Catholics were free to practice their religion, but the Nativists menaced them in many ways. Street preachers would travel across from Manhattan on many weekends, decrying the Pope, while also casting aspersions on Catholics on local street corners. Nativist bands often paraded by the church on South Second, playing the death march, a grim warning of the level of hatred Nativists felt.

Nativism grew in direct proportion to the increase in immigration in the late 1840s and 1850s. In 1849, anti–immigrant forces in New York created the secret Order of the Star-Spangled Banner, and soon after nativists formed lodges in nearly every other major American city, including Williamsburg. Nativists also formed, the secretive "Know Nothing" Party, which was so named because members swore and oath to reveal nothing about the party. As its membership grew in the 1850s, the group slowly abandoned its clandestine character, taking the official name American Party, calling for restrictions on immigration, the exclusion of the foreign-born from voting or holding public office in the United States, and for a 21-year residency requirement for citizenship. The party soon had many members elected to Congress, and nominated a number of candidates for city offices in Williamsburg, which spurred anger amongst its Catholic residents.

The American Party organized nationally throughout the early 1850s under the leadership of James W. Barker, a xenophobic New York City merchant and political leader. The party's platform of preventing immigrants from being elected to make laws and keeping legislative power as the exclusive property of native-born Americans resounded with many xenophobic Williamsburgers.

While Barker appealed to educated New Yorkers, a Manhattan street thug, William Poole, known as Bill the Butcher, provided intimidating muscle on the ground for Nativist politicians. Poole was paid to be a "shoulder hitter" at election time, using gang violence to intimidate pro-immigrant Tammany Hall Democratic voters. For example, on August 26, 1852, he and his gang of Know Nothing Party supporters violently disrupted the election of Democratic Delegates for State and County conventions at an eighth ward polling place. Bill the Butcher became a popular rabble-rouser, especially popular with the city's volunteer fire companies, which were hotbeds of nativism. In 1852, four hundred nativist volunteer firemen crossed the East River on ferries to intervene in a street brawl, fighting for a nativist Williamsburg firehouse battling a local Irish fire company in a pitched battle on Grand Street. The mayor of Williamsburg and the Common Council denounced the incursion, fearing Manhattan Nativists could spark the local religious powder keg.

In 1853, a riot erupted in Williamsburg between the Nativists and the Irish. Two Nativists, who were beaten in an altercation with six Irishmen, returned to the scene of the fight with an angry nativist mob. When the Irishmen made their escape into Peter Quinn's porterhouse on Grand Street, the mob decided to break in and even the score. They began to batter the door with stones, while the policemen who showed up at the scene at first were powerless to quell the violence. The mob quickly succeeded in prying the door open, heaving paving stones into the room, some weighing ten or twelve pounds. Mrs. Quinn was struck in the left side with a stone and hurt badly. Mr. Quinn was also seriously injured when he was hit in the chest by a stone. The Nativists shattered a large mirror standing at the back of the bar with stones. Quinn, in desperation, grabbed a shotgun, firing in the air to scare the mob, but with no effect. The mob made another rush for the door with knives, cart rungs and stones, but were stopped by the policemen, who now blocked the doorway, determined to keep them back. Captain Hunt of the Second Ward squad finally arrived with a group of re-enforcements, putting an end to the disturbance, and probably preventing the loss of life, as the Irishmen in the house had armed themselves with four muskets, ready to shoot their nativist enemies.

Such violence repeated itself with alarming regularity, and soon the violence helped turn Williamsburg into one of the strongholds of the American Party, much to the resentment of the local Irish who were ready to use violence to stop Nativists from voting against them. The American Party ran a slate of candidates for office in 1854, threatening to unleash further violence. Father Malone could have been a voice of reason, but he had been called to Rome before the vote, so he was not present to calm his congregants and diffuse the anger. Violence would soon rear its ugly head.

On election day, a group of four hundred Irishmen loitered outside a polling station on Grand Street, intent on confronting American Party voters. When a poll worker, believed to have nativist sympathies, challenged Irish votes, the long-feared riot broke out. The poll worker, a man called Silkworth, was brutally beaten by the angry mob. Police attempted in vain to clear the streets, but were overwhelmed by the mob, now suddenly armed with clubs, shovels and hoes. A volunteer fireman and deputy sheriff named Harrison was passing by when he came to the aid of Silkworth. Harrison was beaten so severely with a club that he died. Two other men had their skulls broken, but survived.

Harrison's death at the hands of the Irish mob sparked anger and calls for revenge. When it was learned that the victim was a volunteer firemen, Bill the Butcher Poole called for his followers amongst the nativist fire companies to sail over to Williamsburg and exact revenge. Harrison's funeral was to be held locally at Engine Company Number Eight. The funeral was planned to be a huge occasion with all the firehouses in the city sending delegations, increasing the likelihood of violence.

Everyone feared November 8th would be a day of bloodshed. Hundreds of Manhattan Nativists, many of them volunteer firemen, dressed in black armbands, boarded the Williamsburg ferries bent on revenge. They massed on the Williamsburg shoreline, shouting out in unison, "to the church," preparing to burn Fr. Malone's church to the ground. As they headed up Grand Street, they were met by a group of armed Irishmen and a riot ensued. The Irish, armed with clubs and bricks, fought the similarly armed Nativists, but the torch-wielding, nativist mob was too large to contain, and two hundred of them breached the Irish defenses, reached the Catholic church on South Second Street, ready to set it alight. Armed parishioners with rifles had just managed to lock the gates, moving inside the building and loading their weapons, preparing to fight and die in defense of their house of worship. The angry mob shook the gate so violently that the cross, welded to its top, came crashing down, much to the delight of the baying mob. The mob hurled stones through the windows, breaking the stained glass. The church seemed doomed.

Suddenly, the mayor of Williamsburg, William Wall, bravely pushed his way through the menacing mob, addressing them, and amazingly they allowed him to speak. He warned them that the militia was on the way, and would shoot on site anyone attacking the church. He also promised that the men who had killed Harrison would be brought to justice. His bravery, and the threat that the militia would shoot, miraculously averted violence. When three companies of armed militia formed up and took aim at the rioters, the angry mob backed away from the church. The avoidance of bloodshed, and the survival of the church, seemed an act of divine intervention.

The conflict between immigrants and Nativists was serious, but there was another conflict that was coming to a head in America. Within seven years, the religious conflict would abate because the nation would be plunged into Civil War. One of the chief instigators of that conflict would visit Williamsburg before his attempt to start a war. His corpse, with the rope burns from his hanging clearly visible, would be returned to the area and waked on Bedford Avenue. It was a harbinger of the war that would engulf the country.

Chapter Four:
October 18, 1859,
A Martyr Predicts Civil War

Willis Hodges woke up in a cold sweat, violently pulling back the covers of his bed, and a cold blast of air shook him out of his dream state, making him realize he was in Brooklyn, not on his family farm in Prince William County, Virginia. He had just suffered through a re-occurrence of the terrible nightmare that brought him back thirty years to the worst moment of his life, April 24, 1829, when he was only thirteen years old. Still shaken by the awful reality of the dream, he wiped the sweat off his brow, recalling the nightmare's dreadful details. It was a nightmare that had recurred repeatedly over the last thirty years, and he understood that yesterday's terrible news must have reawakened the awful scenes in his subconscious.

In his dream, he was again a thirteen-year-old boy behind the plow and a mule in the fields surrounding the family home when he made out a large group of maybe a hundred white riders emerging from the woods, galloping full speed to the family farm. The Hodges family was a rarity in antebellum Virginia. They were prosperous free black landowners, who were now being targeted because Willis' brother William, twelve years older, had escaped from jail after being arrested on groundless charges of abetting a slave rebellion. Willis ran through the fields as fast as he could, in hopes of warning his mother, but he was too far from the house, and the men on horseback approached too rapidly. His father was away from the farm, leaving Willis as the sole male on the farm. He arrived at the house just after the group of horsemen had dismounted. He tried to run to his mother, but several armed white men prevented him for entering the kitchen where his mother was cooking. He again tried to push into the kitchen, but the white men still pushed the smaller teenager roughly back. In his dream he recalled how one of the group's leaders, Benjamin Woodward, stood menacingly in the family kitchen, and began insulting his mother, calling her "a dammed nigger bitch" before noticing the watch and fine chain that hung around her neck, something unusual for a white woman, and very rare for a black woman, a clear sign of the Hodges' family wealth.

There were five or six other men in the room with Woodard, who began to speak to Willis' mother again: "You look very handsome with a watch and chain, give it here now bitch." His mother was a proud woman, and instead of giving Woodward the watch and chain, she picked up a hickory walking stick, a gift of her husband, quickly giving Woodward two or three quick hard blows to face, which drew blood from his nose, infuriating the white intruder, while rousing the other men in the room into action. They grabbed her, pulled the stick away from her and held her arms down, while Woodward angrily threatened, "You will pay for this." Hodges tried to break free and enter the kitchen, but was still restrained at the door, and made to witness the awful scene that followed. Woodward pinned his mother to the floor and with his thumb began to gouge out his mother's eyes. She screamed at the top of her lungs, "Don't let him put my eyes out!" Woodward continued gouging with sadistic pleasure, while the woman's right eye protruded far from the socket with blood streaming down her face.

Then, Woodward spotted Willis in the doorway, and stopped gouging out his mother's eyes. Woodward walked over to him, grabbing him by the shoulder, pulling out a pistol, as he began pushing him into the yard. He stopped about fifteen paces from the kitchen, put the gun to his head and said, "Tell me where your brother is or I will kill you." Hodges recalled thinking that he would sooner die than reveal any information to this hated white man. He said nothing, and felt a stream of sweat running down his face, while also feeling the cold metal barrel of the gun against the side of his head. Then, he heard the click of the weapon's hammer being pulled back, as Woodward menacingly repeated his threat to kill him if he did not talk. Hodges closed his eyes, not sure if he would ever open them again. Hodges recalled the panic and helplessness he felt. Then, he recalled hearing the loud bang of the pistol, sure that he was dead, but when he opened his eyes he saw that one of the family dogs, which had run up to protect him, lay dying on the ground, a pool of blood running from its head. Woodward pistol whipped him with the weapon and he was knocked to the ground with a hard blow to the head. Woodward then gave the group of mounted white men the order to shoot all the animals. Hodges again heard the firing of several weapons and saw to his horror within a minute all the family dogs, cattle, pigs and chickens lying slaughtered around the barnyard.

It was that day that Hodges made the deep vow that would serve as a catalyst for all his actions and motivate him for the rest of his days. Hodges swore eternal war against slavery, vowing to avenge the wrongs committed against his mother. Hodges had arrived first arrived in Williamsburg in 1836, following his older brother and sisters who had fled persecution as African Americans in the South, even though they were never enslaved. They joined an old, well-established black community in Williamsburg, some of whom were property owners and successful businessmen.

A free African had been one of the original seventeenth century settlers of Bushwick, so there was a long African-American history in the area. Dutch farmers in Brooklyn had owned slaves since the earliest days of New Amsterdam. In 1820, 182 of 934 residents of Williamsburg were African-Americans. Slavery was abolished in New York State in 1827, but by then many local slaveholders had already freed their enslaved workers. Already by 1830, a thriving free black community had arisen in Williamsburg. In 1832, the black community set up their own church, the Zion African Methodist Episcopal Church on North Fourth Street between Bedford Avenue and Berry Street. After the panic of 1837, African Americans bought lots in Williamsburg at fire sale prices after the spectacular burst of the real estate bubble. One of those who bought land was Willis' older brother William, who became a preacher and a grocery store owner. Willis and his brothers were literate, a rarity in the community, so it is not surprising that they quickly became community leaders. Willis was appalled by the low economic status of many in the free black community, and wanted to improve it, so he helped set up the first school for African Americans in Williamsburg in 1841. He and many other African- American residents of Williamsburg also set up safe houses to help freed slaves escape north on the Underground Railroad, but Hodges wanted to do much more than merely help slaves escape. He wanted to eradicate slavery.

Hodges pushed his community to be more militant in demanding their right to vote. In 1841, he and other African-American citizens of Williamsburg made a pledge to fight voting rights discrimination, stating:

> Resolved we the citizens of Williamsburg, feeling the injustice of unequal suffrage under which we labor, do hereby pledge ourselves to use our united exertions to restore an equality of suffrage and not to cease them until the last link of the oppressor's chain is broken.

Willis Hodges had met many white men, but he had only met one white man who had made the same vow to destroy slavery and kept his word. That man was John Brown, and it was his arrest yesterday that had caused Hodges to relive the nightmarish scene of his youth.

Hodges got up out of bed and went to a box beside the fireplace, fetching some newspaper and kindling to light the fire. He retrieved a match from a box in a drawer on his desk, and lit the kindling, softly throwing it on the logs in the fireplace. After a minute or so, flames appeared and the logs began to burn. Soon, the fire warmed the room, and Hodges remembered what he needed to do. He pulled open a lower drawer, in the back of which he found a bundle of letters tied with a bow. He untied the bow, and began to quickly read through the letters, separating them into two piles.

In about a half an hour, Hodges had completed sorting through the letters. He grabbed the larger pile, walked to the fire place, and threw the letters into the fire, watching the paper burn up, lost in thought about the author of the letters: John Brown.

He had known Brown for a decade, but he had always had mixed feelings about him, even though there was no white man to whom he had ever felt closer. Hodges had met hundreds of abolitionists, and though he admired their repugnance at slavery, most were mere orators who were unwilling to fight slavery with more than words. Brown was the one white man who was different, because he was ready to act. Brown saw the issue of slavery more clearly than any other white man: slavery meant war, a holy war, which Brown was ready to fight, and die, in.

Hodges would never have met Brown if he had not felt it was his duty as one of the few literate blacks from the South to reveal the rampant racism and cruelty free African Americans suffered there. He was determined to show the world the sufferings of free blacks in the south, as well as his enslaved brethren. Hodges had spent his own hard earned money, $15 in 1846, to publish a rebuttal in *The New York Sun* to an editorial against dropping the $250 property qualification that prevented most New York Blacks from voting. Hodges recalled how he was infuriated to learn that they had not treated his rebuttal as an editorial, but had treated it as a mere advertisement, sticking it in the back of the newspaper where no one would see it. When he confronted the editor, reminding him of the paper's motto, "The sun shines for all," the racist editor replied, "The sun does not shine for colored men. You must get up your own paper if you want to tell your side of the story."

Most blacks laughed at him, thinking him naive when he told them of his determination to publish a black journal, but he had made the paper a reality, and that was how he first came into contact with Brown, who not only subscribed, but also sent him lists of subscribers. Brown agreed to write for his paper, *The Ram's Horn*, which Hodges named from the book of Joshua, for he hoped to make such a loud blast that the walls of slavery would come down. Brown sent him an excellent piece that Hodges loved, which criticized freed blacks in the North who spoke against slavery, but did little to stop it.

He first met Brown during the hard winter of 1849, when he had left Williamsburg to try and form a free black community in the Adirondack Mountains. The land they were given was so different than the fine soil he had known in Virginia. It was thin, too thin to farm, and the long winters made the growing season short. His fellow settlers were hungry, but Brown not only sent them food, but also came to live besides them. He invited the settlers to his house, where they all sat at one table, a shocking occurrence for many of the black dinner guests. He had never met another white who felt so at ease with his people.

That cold hard winter in the Adirondacks, Hodges started to write his autobiography, often receiving Brown as a guest. During one of these visits, Brown told Hodges of his belief that they needed to do more than speak about abolition, they needed to strike at slavery, instigating a revolt just as Nat Turner had tried unsuccessfully to do in his native Virginia in 1831.

It was his knowledge of fellow black Virginian Turner, and his failed revolt, that always made Hodges question Brown's planned slave revolt. Hodges recalled with horror how they had hanged Turner and his followers, and Hodges thought that the same would happen to Brown. Now, on this cold morning, he knew that his intuition had been right - Brown was going to hang.

Willis Hodges had returned to Williamsburg in 1851 because the black farming venture in the Adirondacks proved to be a debacle. While Hodges had been away in northern New York, a new federal law had dramatically changed the position of free black people in the North, and it would immediately affect one of the members of the Williamsburg black community.

James Hamlet, a free black resident of Williamsburg born in New York, became the first kidnapping victim after passage of the Fugitive Slave Act in 1850. Hamlet was working as a porter in Manhattan when Maryland businessman Gustavas Brown saw him, and falsely claimed that Hamlet was a runaway from his mother's home in Maryland. Hamlet, who lived on South Third Street with his wife and three children, was arrested and sent to Baltimore. His testimony, as a supposed runaway slave, was inadmissible, angering both the free black and white abolitionist communities.

Maryland resident Brown exercised his rights under the Fugitive Slave Act of 1850. Brown authorized a federal official to claim Hamlet, and return him to his mother's Baltimore home. Despite the differences in her testimony, and Hamlet's pleadings and protests of being born a free man, the federal authorities, obligated by Congress' legislation, robbed a husband of his wife, two children and freedom, outraging blacks and their abolitionist allies. Hodges spoke out against the outrage, and helped the community raise the funds to buy Hamlet from bondage. Five hundred blacks jammed a Manhattan church, and together with white abolitionist allies, they raised $800 to free Hamlet. Three days later, thousands of people attended a rally in Manhattan where Hodges spoke, demanding Hamlet's release. When Hamlet came home, Hodges joined the huge celebration of two hundred local blacks, jubilantly escorting Hamlet back to Williamsburg.

Brown had come to Brooklyn in the spring of the year, trying to recruit Hodges and other members of his community to join him in starting the slave revolt, but Hodges demurred, and Brown chided him, asking him why he had grown so lukewarm. Hodges was evasive, and did not tell him his doubts about the Harper's Ferry raid.

Hodges followed news about Brown's trial in the paper, even though he knew his hanging was certain. When he was convicted, Hodges was stunned by his prophecy, "I John Brown am now quite certain that the crimes of this guilty land will never be put away without blood. I had as I now think vainly flattered myself that without much blood it would be done." The night of his hanging, church bells all over Brooklyn tolled in memory of the martyr.

Brown's widow claimed his corpse. Brown had told her in their last meeting that he wanted to be buried on his farm, besides the freed black people he had helped back in 1849. She took his corpse north by train, and it arrived in Brooklyn, where a Court Street undertaker prepared it. Williamsburg abolitionist John Stearns approached the undertaker to have Brown's body waked in his home on Bedford Avenue. Hodges and his brothers were invited to come to Stearns' home, and eulogize Brown. Walking into Stearns' parlor, Hodges was deeply shaken as saw the coffin with Brown's body lying inside. The face had not changed. He noticed his beard, but the bright, intense, righteous eyes were now closed. Hodges knelt in prayer over his friend's corpse, and tried to pray, but his eyes were drawn to the rope burns that were still clearly visible on his neck.

As he prayed for Brown's soul, Brown's words sworn more than a decade before came to Hodges: "Here before God, in the presence of these witnesses for the first time, I consecrate my life to the destruction of slavery."

Hodges could never have imagined how close at hand that destruction was.

Chapter Five:
The Death of the Philanthropist - May 21, 1860

News of his death spread like wildfire around Williamsburg. If one man had embodied all that was noble, self-sacrificing and virtuous in the community, then it was Grahams Polley, and the community was deeply shocked to learn of his passing. He was only Forty-four years old, and he left behind a widow and ten children who would certainly grieve, but they would not grieve alone. The entire old town of Williamsburg would mourn Polley's death. It was regarded a calamity for the entire community.

In the spring of 1860, Williamsburg was a deeply divided community in a deeply divided country. There were rancorous local splits between Republican and Democrat, Protestant and Catholic, abolitionist and supporter of slavery, but for a brief moment those differences were set aside and Williamsburg was united in grief. No one had done more for the old town than Polley. No one had been more civic minded, open-hearted or truly generous than Polley. People recalled his genial manner, kindly smile and utter lack of pretension, but most of all they recalled his amazing charity.

Polley was one of the four or five richest men in the Eastern District, but that did not seem to matter now. It was his complete generosity that people recalled and loved. Born in Manhattan in 1816 into a poor family, Polley came to Williamsburg as a young man, starting his career working as a teenager in a rope works. A man of great energy, Polley was destined to rise. He soon opened his own profitable local rope works. Then, he started an even more profitable business, a distillery that allowed him to purchase several pieces of prime real estate. He even became president of the richest local bank, but it was the money he gave away, not the money he kept, that earned him universal respect. In the economic panic of 1857, he established a grocery store, providing so much credit to his neighbors that he lost $6,000, but Polley felt it was his duty to his neighbors to feed them during those bad economic times, and never once considered closing the unprofitable market.

His death made people pause, and reminded them of their mortality. He had been a vigorous, healthy man in the prime of life only a few years ago. However, he was thrown from his horse in a riding accident, suffering serious internal injuries. Confined to bed, he had suffered for a long period before God, in his mercy, had ended the good man's misery.

His charity was a quiet, unpretentious generosity. All his life, evidences of suffering and distress easily moved him, especially with children. He had once been poor himself, and he never forgot the pain of poverty. He had acquired wealth, but it never changed him. He was never pompous, and always remained a man of a quiet demeanor and simple tastes. His sympathies were with the poor, and he remained open to alleviation of local poverty without regard to race, creed or color. Someone said of him that his heart was never cold, nor his hand closed to the appeal of want or suffering.

He was amazingly generous to his employees, who were totally devoted to him. He paid them when they were sick. He even kept trusted employees who had died on the payroll so that their widows could keep collecting a salary. He gave them gifts at Christmas and Thanksgiving, and helped them in a hundred ways.

The day of his wake was the saddest day Williamsburg had ever seen. No one, not even the oldest people in the area, could remember anything quite like the outpouring of grief his death stirred. There was shock and a pervasive sadness that bound all the residents, regardless of race, religion or social status. Everyone in Williamsburg had loved Grahams Polley, and no one could fathom that he was now gone.

During the days of his wake and funeral, Williamsburg was eerily still. Everyone spoke in hushed tones, and the normal sound of the laughter of children was totally absent. All the area's shops closed as a mark of respect, and black bunting covered many of the houses. The schools flew the flag at half-mast, and the schools he founded were also draped in black bunting. Ministers in all the different houses of worship held him up as an example of a good man, praising his self-lessness and compassion.

All agreed that he was an extraordinary human being, yet here was nothing special in his appearance that marked the greatness of his soul. The man lying in the coffin was only of medium height, stout with a large head and whiskers. He had a pronounced Roman nose that prevented him from being called handsome. His eyes were shut now, but people remembered his clear gray eyes that had shown so much kindness. He hated show or ostentation, and he never wanted his numerous acts of charity publically revealed. Many had wanted to commission a portrait of him, for he

embodied the civic spirit of Williamsburg, but he refused all but one person. He reluctantly agreed to sit
for a portrait for his friend, John Stearns, who painted
his only portrait. Ironically, the canvas was finished
on the very day Polley died, so Stearns was unable to
show the likeness to Polley.

His corpse was sent to the coroner's office, and
then taken home by wagon to be laid in state in a pine
coffin on the lawn in front of his home at Kent Avenue
and North First Street so that the whole town could
pay their respects. All day long, blacks and whites,
Catholics and Protestants and even Jews arrived, pa-
tiently standing in line for over an hour in silence for
the chance to say good-bye to the kind-hearted man.
Rich and poor alike stood dressed in their best attire,
waiting on the long line that strung far down Kent Avenue. No one, however, uttered a word of complaint.
Ten thousand mourners passed by his coffin. His funeral cortege contained more than a hundred and fifty
carriages as his coffin was carried off to Green-Wood
Cemetery.

Although everyone was sad, it was the school children who took his death the hardest. Many of the children brought to his bier wept uncontrollably, for they
knew how much he loved them. Many adults realized
that it was thanks to Polley that local children had re-

ceived an education, and they were keenly aware of the difference he had made in the lives of Williamsburg's children.

His greatest legacy was the local schools he founded. Williamsburg was no longer an independent city, having merged with the City of Brooklyn in 1855. Now it was known as the Eastern District, but today there were memories of the old city, and of the man who was regarded as the most selfless citizen of the old town. He embodied the spirit of the old city, the personification of its generosity and concern for others. He donated land for a school. He also donated the lot for the local firehouse on Kent and North Fifth Street, becoming the treasurer of the firehouse, and its secret patron.

Williamsburg could make one claim to greatness Brooklyn could not, and it was Polley's greatest legacy. Williamsburg set up free primary schools eight years before Brooklyn, thanks to Polley. Polley did not have the chance to get much schooling himself, but he determined that the children of Williamsburg would not suffer for want of education, so his great civic act was becoming the patron of the local primary schools.

Polley was the most important trustee on the Williamsburg schools when it was still an independent city. Williamsburg had four primary schools, each founded and endowed by Polley. He spent lavishly on the schools, giving the principals of all the schools free reign to spend what they needed to educate the children. He even believed that black children should have the chance to get an education, and he generously funded their school, a rare belief in racist antebellum America. Teachers loved him fervently. When the teachers were sick and could not work, he still paid their wages. He hosted a yearly dinner for the district's teachers, thanking them for their work.

He was most generous, however, to children. He secretly bought poor children shoes, gloves and winter coats. He spent large sums of money for books, and every year in May he funded a festival at his personal expense that the children adored. He funded sleigh, ferry and stage coach excursions for each school. He even purchased paintings, pianos and organs for the schools, but never wanted credit, always refusing any public acknowledgment of his largess.

Fifty years after his passing, the students in Polley's schools recalled with great fondness the patron of Williamsburg schools. Two of the grief-stricken children who passed his coffin that may day would go on to leave a legacy thanks to the education they received in one of the schools Polley endowed: Public School number seventeen. Eugene Armbruster would

write an important history of the Eastern District, recalling until the end of his life how the education he
received changed his life. State Senator Patrick McCarren, unlike many other Irish working-class Brooklyn children, learned to read and write in P.S. 17. He
would enter politics, becoming a lawyer and one of
the most influential lawmakers in the state. One day
he would use the intelligence he first honed in P.S. 17
to acquire Williamsburg its bridge. Polley never could
have imagined the good fruit that grew from the seeds
of generosity he had planted so long ago.

Chapter Six:
Another Sugar Empire Rises

In 1856, Fredrick Havemeyer often took the ferry across the East River, making numerous visits to the bustling Williamsburg shoreline, hoping to scout out a location for the sugar refinery he planned to establish on the Brooklyn side of the river. While the establishment of a Brooklyn refinery by the Havemeyer family was a new era for Williamsburg, it was merely another chapter in the long history of sugar in the Americas. The history of the new world and the history of sugar cane are so intertwined that it is impossible to separate the two.

Havemeyer probably could never have imagined in 1856 the wealth, power and extent of the empire he was setting up, but it was only the latest of many empires that were built on sugar wealth. The Spanish Empire had grown wealthy from its control of the sugar trade. Christopher Columbus had once been a sugar buyer before he became an explorer. On his second voyage to the "New World" in 1493, Columbus brought sugarcane to grow in the Caribbean, shaping the economic and social destiny of the islands for centuries.

Columbus himself was unable to establish a successful sugar plantation, but others soon did. The tropical climate and volcanic soils provided by the Caribbean proved to be the perfect environment for sugarcane cultivation. Cuba, in 1856 still a Spanish colony, was destined to become the world's leading producer of sugar and the major provider of Havemeyer sugar. Portugal also set up vast sugar plantations in Brazil, making fortunes for Portuguese sugarcane plantation owners. Tons of raw sugar from all these places would arrive for decades in Williamsburg.

In many cases sugarcane became the predominant export crop for many Caribbean islands, a dependence that remained for centuries, and one the Havemeyer family business not only took advantage of, but also even increased. If Caribbean islands and Brazil were dependent on sugar, then their economies were totally dependent on slaves who were stolen in Africa by the tens of millions and cruelly brought to the new world. Misunderstanding the harshness of sugar slavery, planters expected that they would not have to import many slaves because they mistakenly believed these Africans would reproduce and their children would also cut cane. Unfortunately, the life of a sugarcane plantation slave was so harsh that life expectancy was only two years. Slaves did not live long enough to reproduce themselves, so the slave trade continued illegally even into the late nineteenth century in Cuba and Brazil.

The Havemeyers grew rich from exploiting the sugar grown and harvested, by slaves. Although slavery in the United States ended in 1865, it continued until 1886 in Cuba, and only ended in 1888 in Brazil. Many of the tons of raw sugar the Havemeyers brought to Williamsburg waterfront were the products of slaves. Familiar with every aspect of sugar production, the Havemeyers also had to know the danger of cutting sugarcane, and how exhausted slaves missed the cane, cutting off fingers and even hands. However, they never focused on the ethics of the sugar business. The Havemeyers intended to get rich from sugar, and they closed their eyes to the evil sugar cane cultivation engendered. Even after the emancipation of slaves, the descendants of these slaves toiled in inhuman and dangerous conditions for barely subsistence wages.

Sugar acted as the chief agricultural commodity in the international trading system known as the triangle trade. The Caribbean and Brazil shipped huge amounts of raw sugar to Europe, and later to America. Europe sent cheap manufactured goods to Africa. Tens of millions of Humans were sucked into the evil system and shipped to the Americas as slaves. By the mid-1700s, sugar output was still relatively small, and it was still an expensive luxury known as "white gold." Governments loved sugar because it was highly taxed, bringing millions of dollars into government treasuries. Sugar profits, built on slave labor, poured into Europe, funding the industrial revolution, allowing them to become dominant players in the world economy.

By the seventeenth century, sugar was the most valuable agricultural commodity in the world, and the major refiners of sugar were the Dutch. It is little wonder that their colony of New Amsterdam became involved in the sugar trade, trading with Dutch colonies in the West Indies. When New Amsterdam became New York, the sugar trade not only continued, but even grew in wealth.

The sugar trade helped to build New York, making it into a rich commercial center. In the eighteenth century, when New York was still a tiny trading post, sugar became the world's leading commodity. New York became rapidly integrated into the world sugar trade. By about 1720, half the ships in New York harbor were passing to or from the sugar islands. New

York farmers planted food that was exported to the Caribbean on those ships. New York created a nascent ship-building industry, building ships to make the journey south to the sugar islands. One in four New Yorkers in eighteenth century New York was a sailor, and the activity of the port of New York reflected the rhythms of the Caribbean sugar trade. From November to January, New York had a bustling harbor with many American vessels headed south as ships brought food to the Caribbean, returning with hulls laden with raw sugar, much of which was turned into rum. The trade died in the winter, but resumed from April to June as mariners hurried to beat the hurricane season. The city, however, still did little refining itself.

In 1730, New York merchant Nicholas Bayard realized that there was an untapped local market for refined sugar, even if its high price made it a luxury item only the rich could afford. Setting up a sugarhouse required a lot of capital, but Bayard was rich enough to afford it. He erected a house for refining all sorts of sugar, and he procured an experienced baker for his sugarhouse who understood the poorly grasped process of refining raw brown sugar into refined white sugar. Sugar production was extremely crude and slow before the revolution, but quite lucrative.

The American Revolution was partly fought over

sugar. British mercantilist laws, when enforced, prevented the thirteen colonies from trading with the Spanish and French Caribbean, and the strict enforcement of these laws was one of the grievances that led to the Declaration of Independence. By the time of the revolution, Manhattan had a few sugarhouses, many of which were used as prisons for American patriots.

Other New Yorkers followed Bayard into the sugar refining business, and they included some of the most prominent families in New York City history, including the Van Cortland, Livingston and Roosevelt families. The process these sugarhouses employed was highly unscientific, time consuming and labor-intensive. Sugar was wetted, heated, and then filtered into cone-shaped molds. Much of the sugar was lost in the process, and only the sugar at the top of the cone produced was white. In the years after the Revolution, science had had little effect on the process of making sugar, which was considered more of an intuitive art than a scientific process.

The history of the Havemeyer family was so connected to sugar refining that it was hard to think of the first without immediately thinking of the other. The Havemeyers were already an established, wealthy sugar clan by the time Fredrick Havemeyer decided to set up a Williamsburg refinery. The Havemeyer family had started a family sugar refining business in Germany in the eighteenth century. In 1799 there were still few men in New York who had mastered the art of "baking" raw sugar into white refined sugar, and such experts were very much in demand. Word reached the city's Seaman Sugarhouse about a talented young German sugarhouse manager in London, the world capital of sugar refining, who was willing to relocate to New York, so the Seaman firm invited William Havemeyer to manage its refinery. Two years later, William invited his brother Fredrick, who had also apprenticed in London, to join him in New York. The brothers could never have imagined they were destined to start a firm that would become the world's largest sugar refiner.

Both brothers had mastered the difficult art of refining sugar, becoming experts at boiling sugar. The first step in refining sugar in those early days of baking sugar was to place the raw sugar into a kettle and melt it in a white lime solution that would neutralize the impurities and prevent fermentation. Then they filtered it with bags to try to remove as much of the foreign matter as they could from the raw sugar. The solution was further cleared with bullock's blood, albumen and clay. Finally, the mixture was re-boiled until it crystalized in a conical-shaped sphere known as a sugar loaf. Lumps from the cylinder were cut for individual customers, most of whom were well-to-do New Yorkers.

It took real skill to master the refining process. If it boiled too long, the sugar turned brown and lost taste. Success in refining sugar meant converting raw sugar into refined sugar with a minimum loss of glucose, but in those early, pre-technology days a lot of lost sugar was lost in the refining process. A skilled refiner like William Havemeyer might get fifty pounds of white refined sugar from a hundred pounds of raw sugar.

The two brothers married American women and started families; however, they knew that the real money was not in working for someone else, but in starting their own sugarhouse. They left the Seaman Sugarhouse and started to build their own sugar-house. In 1807, they opened the Havemeyer Brothers Sugar Refinery on Van Dam Street with only four or five employees. The two-story sugarhouse was only thirty-five feet wide, and houses in the back served as homes for the brothers' families. The location of the sugarhouse was ideal, since it was not far from the docks so that shipments of raw Caribbean sugar could easily reach their sugarhouse.

The two Havemeyer brothers trained their sons to inherit the family business. The sons served four-year apprenticeships in which they learned every aspect of the trade, and eventually the two German immigrants handed the business over to them. Their sons would apply what they had learned in their apprenticeships, yet these sons, Fredrick Havemeyer, and his cousin William, would achieve extraordinary things their fathers could scarcely have dreamed of. William would enter politics and get elected three times as the mayor of New York City. Cousin Fredrick would become one of America's first millionaires, build the world's largest refinery and hand a sugar empire over to his sons.

Chapter Seven:
Steam and Sugar

In 1807, the same year that Fredrick Christian Havemeyer was born behind the Van Dam Street sugar house his father had just set up, inventor Robert Fulton successfully sailed his steamship the *Clermont* against the tide and up the Hudson River, making the round-trip to Albany in a record shattering thirty-two hours, the same trip that took a sailing schooner four days. Water travel was instantaneously revolutionized, and a new steam age in American history was inaugurated.

Steam-powered ferries opened up the East River shoreline in Brooklyn for development, and started the transformation of Williamsburg from isolated agricultural hamlet to industrial city. Thanks to steam-powered ferryboats, the trip to Williamsburg was transformed from a slow, often arduous sail into a fast trip across the East River. Williamsburg developers like Woodhull and Morrell had failed in large part due to the difficulties presented by slow ferries powered only by a team of horses. Fast steam-powered ferry journeys to Williamsburg signaled to investors that the area was suddenly a potential real estate goldmine. In 1827, when the first steam-powered ferry service opened, it made the quick trip to Lower Manhattan from Williamsburg a reality, spurring development and encouraging feverish Williamsburg land speculation. In 1836, when the Grand Street steam ferry opened, commuters could then reach Manhattan with only a fifteen-to-twenty minute trip. The fast commute made living in Williamsburg and working each day in Manhattan, a reality. Naturally, the population soared, and Williamsburg grew by 1855 into the seventh largest city in America.

Steam engines would radically transform land travel as well. In 1829, Britain's George Stephenson successfully designed the first steam railroad locomotive. The following year, New Yorker Peter Cooper built his Tom Thumb engine, which powered a locomotive on the Baltimore and Ohio Railroad. An age of rail commuter travel and rail freight transport was born. The Tom Thumb and the *Clermont* revolutionized business. In the new steam age, railroads and steamboats linked markets that up until then were too far apart to do business. Businesses could engage in commerce at distances that were unthinkable only a few years previously. Markets were transformed from local to regional, and even national, during the 1830s and 1840s. Sugar could reach new markets where it had never been sold before.

Steam power and technological advances were also beginning to effect sugar refining. Slowly, sugar refining was becoming a scientific process, not a matter of human intuition. In 1812, Edward Howard patented the vacuum pan, forever changing the sugar-boiling process. The vacuum pan removed the air from the boiling vat, allowing boiling to occur at much lower temperatures. Also, once the process started in the vacuum pan it continued on its own, so there was a far reduced need for fuel and water. Additionally, the vacuum pan took the guesswork out of sugar boiling, and refiners knew exactly when the sugar was ready to boil. Because the boiling occurred at a lower temperature, the crystals did not burn as they had previously done under older methods, and the sugar mix did not burn or caramelize. Output increased, and profits soared, after the introduction of the vacuum pan. The vacuum pan also eliminated many of the problems with discoloration that had previously plagued refiners. A refiner could now produce in a month the same amount of sugar he refined in a year, thanks to this revolutionary device. The price of sugar dropped precipitously, and consumption soared.

The introduction of bone black also improved sugar refining. Previously, much of the refined sugar had ended up brown, but now using bone black as a filter removed far more of the impurities from the liquid sugar mix, leaving a far whiter and purer refined sugar than the previous method of filtration. The demand for bone black created an army of scavengers who would collect the bones, and then bring them to refineries to be sold.

Fredrick Christian Havemeyer and his cousin William Havemeyer were groomed to take over and run the family sugar business. The first generation American Havemeyer cousins were trained in the old German apprentice system to learn the business. The brothers both had sired large families, and they had chosen two of their sons to run the business after they retirement.

The cousins were both similar in their love of academic learning. Both had a college education, extremely rare for sugar refiners of their day. William was tutored privately, and entered Columbia University at age fifteen in 1819, graduating four years later. His cousin Fredrick Christian was also tutored at home, following his cousin into Columbia University at age fourteen, two years after his cousin was admitted. Fredrick Christian only finished two years of his study because his father had determined that it was time he learned the sugar business by becoming an apprentice in the family business alongside his older cousin William.

In 1823, the two cousins were apprenticed in the family business for five years in the German manner so that they learned every aspect of sugar refining. They not only knew the commercial aspects of the business, but they could also fire up the kilns, shovel in the right amount of the raw sugar and fix the vacuum pans. They wore overalls, and were treated exactly the same as the other sugar house employees.

In 1828, the founders of the family business retired, passing the firm onto their sons who after serving their apprenticeship were deemed ready to run the business. The immigrant brothers had run their business for sixteen years, and by the time of their retirement both had become very rich men. They were old for their day: William and Fredrick were fifty-three and forty-nine years old respectively.

The plant the two cousins were training in was tiny in comparison to the sugar refinery Fredrick Christian would build thirty years later in Williamsburg, employing only twelve men and producing a mere 100,000 pounds of sugar annually, importing most of the raw sugar they refined from Cuba or Brazil. The refined sugar that they turned out was still only shaped in conical molds into loaves, and was such a luxury item that it was locked up to prevent the help from sampling it. Like their fathers, both cousins lived behind the small refinery, married young and had large families, each cousin fathering ten kids.

Sugar refining, though, was in a state of rapid transition. It was changing from the small-scale production of skilled artisans into industrial refining in plants on a huge scale. The leading industrial center for sugar refining was London, where for the first time steam power was replacing human and animal labor in refining sugar. Huge industrial sugar concerns, powered by steam engines, arose in Britain.

Soon, a New York firm also began to utilize steam power in its sugar production. In 1832, the Stuart brothers introduced steam power into their refinery in the Lower West Side of Manhattan. Their father had started as a sugar refiner and confectioner, but died, leaving the business, and his debts, to his sons. At age twenty-one Robert Stuart took charge of the plant and his brother Alexander joined him. Their sugarhouse was the only sugar refinery in the city supplied with gas, with which they planned to generate the steam. Everyone, including the two Havemeyer cousins, predicted their failure. One day, as Alexander was supervising the installation of a huge steam boiler, William Havemeyer, walking by on the street, saw the scene and cried out, warning his rival, "Don't do it, it will ruin you."

Havemeyer's warning turned out to be unfounded, and by 1834, the two brothers had been so successful that they patented their steam refining process. They realized a fourfold increase in output thanks to steam, and their daily output rose from 3,000 pounds daily to 12,000 pounds a day. The Stuarts also applied steam power to other labor-intensive tasks in the plant, such as lifting huge quantities of raw sugar to the top of the plant to begin the refining process. When the Stuart brothers exhibited their patented method the same year at the American Institute Fair, their sparkling white sugar crystals made the public gasp in wonder and admiration, while all of New York's other refiners envied them, realizing that their methods of refining without steam power were, for the most part, obsolete.

The Stuarts were able to produce greater quantities of refined sugar far more cheaply than other refiners, so they could price their sugar much cheaper than their competitors. With profits rolling in, the brothers reinvested in expanding their plant. They built a monster, new state-of-the-art refinery at the corner of Greenwich and Read Streets in Manhattan that stretched over four lots, dwarfing their competitors' refineries. Their new plant was eight stories tall with eight massive steam boilers that consumed an amazing 8,000 tons of anthracite coal each year. The invention of a granulating machine in the 1830s allowed refiners to dry sugar far more rapidly, increasing output, while cutting refining time. The plant could refine an amazing 1,100 pounds of sugar every eleven and a half minutes.

By 1853, the Stuart refinery dominated the American refining industry, turning out 40,000,000 tons of refined sugar annually, while employing three hundred men. Their only rival was the East Boston Sugar Company run by John Brown, who had gone to England to master steam powered refining, but his plant only turned out 25,000,000 pounds of sugar annually. By the 1850s, sugar refining was the city's largest industry, turning out an incredible 190,000,000 pounds of sugar, making New York one of the world's leading markets for world sugar

It might have seemed to keen observers in 1853 that Brown or the Stuart brothers were destined to dominate the sugar refining business; however, the Havemeyer family would emerge as the dominant New York sugar refiners. They would soon construct a rival sugarhouse, adopting modern refining methods, and achieving market dominance thanks in large part to the many advantages of their Williamsburg waterfront location.

Chapter Eight:
Sugar Refining Arrives in
Williamsburg

By 1854, America was entering a new industrial age, and the independent city of Williamsburg was one of its fastest-growing urban areas. The following year, Williamsburg gave up its status as an independent city, merging along with neighbors Bushwick and Greenpoint into the city of Brooklyn. The new area of Brooklyn created by the merger was called the Eastern District, and its geography made it the perfect place for the sugar industry to relocate from Manhattan. In 1856, Fredrick Havemeyer began a sugar business that would dwarf all the other businesses on the East River shore of the new Eastern District.

Havemeyer, aged forty-nine, was the kind of rich New Yorker who usually no longer worked and lived off his investments, but Fredrick was very different than his sugar refining peers. The aristocratic, genteel Havemeyer was not necessarily handsome, but he had a distinguished, scholarly air. He had a large forehead and a large Roman nose that dominated his face. He was tall and lanky with large hands and a long face, which gave him a peculiar kind of dignity. Even though he had retired from the business and was no longer active in refining, Fredrick Christian Haveymeyer was still widely regarded as the outstanding authority on refining sugar in the United States.

Unlike other refiners of his age and class, Havemeyer was looking to re-enter the sugar refining business he had retired from more than fifteen years previously. In 1856, there were few 49-year-olds in the refining business, and none who were looking to undertake the huge stress of building and managing a vast modern refinery. To the men of his day Fredrick Havemeyer was already an old man, but Havemeyer was still very vigorous, and he keenly wanted to re-establish the family refining dynasty not for himself, but more for his four young sons who needed careers. Sugar refining was already established as the Havemeyer family business, one that he intended to pass on to the next generation.

In 1841, having already grown rich from his years in the family firm, he had initially retired from active management of the Van Dam Street refinery, passing control over to his younger brother Dieter, but retaining his share in the profits. He invested a lot of the money he had made into bank shares. Fredrick sat for many years on the Board of Directors of National City Bank. His cousin William also retired as a wealthy man from the firm a year later, similarly leaving management of his half of the firm to his brother Albert. Fredrick's decision was impacted by the death of his father, who had started the family business. As executor of his father's will, and guardian of his widowed mother, Fredrick had many obligations and enough wealth not to work.

By 1856, his brother Dieter had also passed away, and none of his other brothers had an interest in refining sugar, leaving Fredrick's half of the refinery without a manager. Fredrick's sons were still far too young and inexperienced to take over the firm, so it fell to Havemeyer to revive the family business. In the years since his retirement from the family business, Fredrick's cousin William had become active in the Democratic Party's Tammany Hall, which nominated him for mayor in 1845. Havemeyer was elected by a wide margin and served a one-year mayoral term. During William's administration, New York City's Police Department was founded. William also used his money to enter banking and investing. In addition to his political career and banking, William had sired ten children, so he was far too occupied to re-enter the partnership with his cousin.

During his fifteen-year hiatus, Fredrick Christian Havemeyer had seen the folly of his warning the Stuart brothers against using steam power in refineries. Refining sugar was no longer an art, but instead was a technical, highly complex industrial operation. Two years before his father's death in 1839, his aged father had shown the vigor in the Havemeyer genes by sailing back to Europe to visit London, where he had apprenticed in the sugarhouse before rising to manager of it. The old man also visited Germany, the land of his birth. Old Fredrick claimed that he saw more of London during his visit than he had in all his years working there. He must have also witnessed the changes taking place in sugar refining, and reported to his son on the massive industrialization that was occurring in London, where sugar was refined in state-of-the-art plants with cutting-edge technology. Old Havemeyer also saw the same mechanization in the state-of-the-art German refineries when he visited the country of his birth.

Six years after his father's death in 1847, Fredrick, having wound up his father's affairs, and with a lot of inherited money in his pocket, decided to make his own grand tour of Europe. Although he was happy to see the sights, there was far more practical purpose in his visit. Fredrick wanted to inspect mechanized European sugar refineries to study the new industrial techniques they were using to refine sugar, so he visited refineries in England and Germany. His trip convinced him that European methods were much more productive than his firm's obsolete refining techniques. He became convinced that the refiner who integrated these new technologies into sugar production would grow rich and dominate the American market.

Also in 1847, the Havemeyers invited William Moller, a rich and successful New York refiner, to join the firm. Moller brought additional capital that allowed the firm to build a huge third building that towered ten stories above the street. The new building contained updated technology, including vacuum pans and granulators, but it still used many of the same methods the German immigrant founders had used at the turn of the century. By the middle of the 1850s, the Van Dam Street refinery was clearly obsolete.

During his retirement, Fredrick had moved into a house befitting a man of his wealth and station, and large enough to accommodate his wife and ten children. He had a large brownstone built for himself at 193 West Fourteenth Street, which featured unheard of luxuries for the day, including central heat and running water. The house was on the newly designed Union Square. His mother and cousin William also settled near the square. Then, suddenly, Havemeyer suffered a grievous shock when in 1851 his wife suddenly died, leaving him alone to raise his large family. Perhaps her untimely death encouraged him to forget his sorrow by re-entering sugar refining.

Refining sugar was by 1856 a capital-intensive industrial endeavor, requiring huge amounts of space and vast amounts of complicated machinery. The cost and enormous scale of sugar refining had driven many of the smaller players out of the industry, but those that remained could make huge profits. The city had ten steam powered refineries, and the cost of setting up a new steam refinery was steep, costing $500,000 to $800,000; however, utilizing the new technology, refiners could turn out in a moth they previously produced in an entire year. The phenomenal growth of Manhattan had made acquiring land for a new refinery there prohibitive, so Havemeyer began to search for a site for his new refinery in Williamsburg, where space was readily available and costs were far cheaper.

There were a number of advantages to building his refinery in Williamsburg. There were vacant waterfront sites where the plant could be constructed, and the shoreline had deep drafts, allowing cargo ships to dock right at the refinery piers, while also permitting sugar to be directly unloaded from cargo ships. There was also a savings on the transportation costs of carting the massive amounts of sugar to an inland refinery. In 1854, a new law was passed that allowed imported goods like raw sugar to be stored not in government customs houses, but in privately bonded warehouses, removing the costly necessity of having to carry the sugar to the customs house to pay import duties. New York City's unmatched transportation facilities, along with the Erie Canal, gave it an unbeatable competitive advantage in transportation costs. Simply put, the Havemeyers, with their Williamsburg location, could obtain a greater volume of sugar faster and at a lower cost than anyone else, so building along the East River waterfront offered them a massive advantage over their competitors.

Fredrick Havemeyer envisioned building the largest and most technologically advanced refinery in the world, and he needed a technical expert who could build the plant and manage the complicated machinery that the plant contained. In 1857, he sent his second son Theodore to Germany to learn how to construct the new plant and to install and manage the massive machines required to refine sugar on an industrial scale.

Havemeyer needed partners to provide capital for the great expense that building his new refinery would entail. At first, Frederick, partnered with his nephew John C. Havemeyer and refiner Charles Bertrand, began operating a small refinery in Williamsburg. The company was known as Havemeyer & Bertrand, but the partners argued, and the firm soon dissolved. Then, he formed a partnership with his oldest son George, who had been groomed to follow in his refining footsteps, and another successful refiner, Dwight Townsend. The partners leased a large warehouse on South Third Street, and planned to build a refinery that would make all others obsolete. The new refinery would be revolutionary. It was designed to turn out a jaw dropping 300,000 pounds a day, as much as all the other sugar refineries could produce in a month. Additionally, the sugar produced would be whiter and cheaper than any on the market.

By 1860, the new refinery was finished. Theodore had worked twelve hours a day, seven days a week, overseeing its construction. It was a massive seven-story building with rectangular windows and shutters. There was also pair of single-story structures for storage with round-arched window openings and a

freestanding chimney that dwarfed the church steeples that once formed the area's skyline. It seemed
that nothing would interfere with business. The handsome eldest son George was anointed to follow in the
family tradition and become the "Sugar King" who
would grow wealthy and dominate the American market, but war and fate would intervene, smashing those
plans. A tragic accident would occur, which years later
people would claim was part of the curse on the Havemeyer family.

Chapter Nine:
Early Civil War Years

In 1859, while Fredrick Havemeyer was expanding his new Williamsburg refinery, his cousin William was seeking election again as a Democratic candidate for mayor of New York after more than a decade out of office. The issue of slavery had grown in importance during his years out of office, and now divided New York, even amongst Democrats who generally supported the South, opposing interference in the matter of slavery. Havemeyer was nominated by Tammany Hall to run against Democratic candidate Fernando Wood. The two candidates most glaring difference was on the issue of slavery, which hung like a pall over the country. Havemeyer admitted that slavery was an evil, but he wanted to find common ground with the South, and avoid splitting the country. His opponent Wood was a demagogue, and an unapologetic supporter of the South and slavery, who knew that the New York

Irish feared free blacks would compete against them for jobs. A race-baiter, Wood pandered to the fears of Irish working class stating, "Until we have provided and cared for the oppressed laboring man in our own midst, we should not extend our sympathy to the laboring men of other states." The local Irish supported Wood, and it proved to be the difference. Havemeyer narrowly lost to Wood 30,000 to 27,000 votes.

In 1860, Havemeyer announced his support for the pro-slavery Stephen Douglass, the Democratic nominee for president of the United States, whom the South supported. His cousin, Fredrick Christian Havemeyer, also supported Douglass, as did most of the business community, which feared the horrible economic consequences that war would bring. Bankers feared war because they had accepted plantations, and the slaves who worked, them as collateral for loans. A New York merchant summed up what the Havemeyers and other New York businessmen thought, telling an abolitionist his feelings about the possibility of war:

> We are not such fools as not to know that slavery is a great evil... but... there are millions of dollars due from southerners to the merchants and mechanics alone, the payment of which would be jeopardized by any rupture between the North and the South.

We cannot afford, sir, to let you and your associates endeavor to overthrow slavery."

For sugar refiners like Havemeyer, a war would have many negative consequences. The first negative effect on the sugar business would be cutting off the Louisiana sugar crop from Northern refiners, which would limit supply, driving the price of raw sugar up steeply. Secondly, war would remove millions of Southern consumers from the market, dampening business and reducing profits.

Pro-abolitionist Brooklyn differed greatly from pro-slavery Manhattan. Brooklyn showed much more support for Abraham Lincoln and the Republican Party, which opposed the spread of slavery and the Fugitive Slave Act. Protestant ministers in Brooklyn, like the famous Henry Ward Beecher, railed against slavery. Many Brooklynites even opened their homes as stations in the Underground Railroad. Brooklyn's immigrants, however, were split. The large German community was solidly Republican and anti-slavery, while the Irish in Brooklyn, like those in Manhattan, supported the anti- abolitionist Democrats.

In 1860, thirteen-year-old Patrick McCarren heard news of Abraham Lincoln's election. A first generation Irish immigrant, McCarren was well aware of the fact

that, unlike most of their neighbors, the Irish community supported the Democratic Party's candidate Stephen Douglas and slavery. Although just a boy, he was
interested in politics, and knew that war loomed when
Republican Abraham Lincoln was elected president.

McCarren was awakened the morning of April 13,
1861 by the tolling of every church bell in Williamsburg. Running out onto the streets, he inquired why
all the church bells were peeling. He was told that
the Rebels had attacked Fort Sumter, and the North
would fight to preserve the Union. That day he walked
around Williamsburg noticing that many of his Protestant neighbors had hung the stars and stripes out
of the window, but he also noticed that most Irish did
not hang out the flag because few of them supported a
war to end slavery. Soon those differences on slavery
and the war would lead to open conflict on the streets
of New York.

McCarren and the entire community, however, were
shocked when they saw the American flag flying from
the steeple of Saints Peter and Paul Catholic Church
on South Second. Father Malone must have angered
many in his congregation by using the church steeple
to show his support for the keeping the Union together. The following Sunday he further angered some in
his congregation by preaching his support for the war

from the altar. Although many of the Irish were angered by Malone's support of the union cause, many in the Protestant community were pleasantly surprised, and commended Malone for his patriotism at this dark hour. Malone's church became the first American Catholic church ever to fly the stars and stripes, sending an unmistakable signal of the church's support of the Union to the community. The flag remained flying over the church for four years until the end of the war, which finally helped to gain the congregation acceptance into the community.

Williamsburg, like much of the rest of the North, was angry about the Confederate attack at Fort Sumter, and a wave of patriotism engulfed the community. A mass meeting attended by 50,000 Brooklyn residents was held to rally support for the union. One of the most eloquent and enthusiastic pro-Union speakers was Father Malone, whose words convinced many Catholic young men to register in the army and fight for the Union. Protestant, Jewish and Catholic Williamsburgers all volunteered for service after Abraham Lincoln naively issued a call for 75,000 volunteer soldiers who would serve for only ninety days to crush the rebellion.

A number of young men who would play big roles in local history volunteered to fight. Jeremiah Meserole, a rich patrician who was descended from the original Williamsburg settlers, left his job in a Bedford Avenue surveying firm, and volunteered for the 7th Regiment. After his three-month enlistment, he returned home, and helped establish the 47th regiment, which was made up of local Williamsburg and Greenpoint men. Twenty-year-old Sam Collyer, already renowned locally for his boxing skills, joined the 139th Infantry. Irish-born volunteer fireman Martin Short, an apprentice carpenter working at North Second and Driggs, joined the 73rd New York under Tammany Hall politician, General Dan Sickles. The 73rd was a Zouave regiment, made up of many New York volunteer firemen, famous for its fashionable uniforms and impressive drill style. The elegant uniform worn by this regiment, and much admired by Brooklyn ladies, consisted of a dark-blue chasseur jacket with light-blue trim and light-blue trefoils on each sleeve, sky-blue chasseur trousers with two white stripes down each leg, brown leather gaiters, a light-blue kepi with a dark-blue band and dark-blue piping, and a red Zouave fez with a blue tassel as a fatigue cap. Former Williamsburg Mayor, Dr. Clayton Berry, one of the richest men in the area, also enlisted as medical officer. Joe Sprague Star pitcher of the local baseball team, the Eckford Club, would also enlist.

One young man desperate to join was the oldest son of Fredrick Havemeyer, twenty-four-year-old George Havemeyer, who wanted to join his friends who had enlisted in the New York 14th, another Zouave brigade. The soldiers in the 14th wore elegant French-style uniforms with baggy red trousers that gave them their nickname, "The Red Devils." George pleaded with his father to be allowed to join, but his father was deaf to his entreaties, angrily reminding him that he was building a refinery that George would one day run. His father rebuked him saying:

> The people want to hear nothing, but the fife and drum, but I hope that you are going to become a smart businessman and not such a silly goose as to be seduced from the duty to our family by the declarations of bun-combed speeches. It is only Greenhorns who enlist. You can learn nothing in the army. In time you may learn that a man may be a patriot without risking his life or sacrificing his health. There are plenty of other lives less valuable than yours that can be sacrificed for the country.

George and his brother Theodore were apprenticed in the traditional family way to learn every aspect of the business. Their brother-in-law, Charles Senff was also brought into the firm to help build and manage the massive plant. They worked together every day from seven to seven, and often worked all night long. It did not take Theodore long to master every job and every aspect of the plant, because he had largely built it himself. Theodore quickly became, like his father, one of the most knowledgeable sugar refiners in the world.

George reluctantly assented to his father's wishes, though he pined to don a uniform and fight the Rebels. George's request to enlist had hurt Fredrick. In the old man's eyes, everything that he was doing in setting up the refinery at his age was in the interest of his children, most of all in George's interest, because he, as the oldest son, would manage it one day. Although his son worked as hard as his brother Theodore, it was clear to the father that he still harbored the silly dream of wearing a uniform and winning glory on the battlefield. Fredrick, however, consoled himself that in time George would recognize his folly, and understand why he had forbidden his son's enlistment.

One day, the father instructed his son George to inspect a large crank that was not turning properly. George went to the edge of the catwalk and leaned over to look at the mechanism, when suddenly his clothing got caught in the crank of a large machine. The great wheel pulled him over the edge of the catwalk and he fell, calling out as he descended. His father raced over to see that George had fallen four floors. He rushed like a madman down the stairs, screaming and attracting a crowd. When he arrived at the floor where his son landed, he could tell in the eyes of the workmen that George was dead. His son had landed headfirst, and his broken skull was still oozing blood. Fredrick cradled his son in his arms while wailing in grief, still unable to grasp that he lay holding the corpse of his oldest son.

For months, Fredrick was inconsolable. He had forbidden George from entering the army to protect him because he feared that like so many young men, he might return from the war a corpse. It was the bitterest of ironies that instead George had died in the factory his father had intended to leave for him. In time, he realized that he still had three other sons to whom he would pass the refinery. Fredrick Havemeyer was overcome by emotion each time he entered the refinery. He could not help but think about the crank and the awful accident. The memory of the accident haunted him for the rest of his life.

Even in wartime people love amusements. Like many young boys from the Eastern District, Patrick McCarren had fallen in love with Brooklyn's most popular pastime, baseball, even to point of playing it on Sunday and violating the blue laws, which made such activities illegal. The game was played in other parts of America, but nowhere was it loved as it was on the Eastern shore of Long Island. Brooklyn had more teams than anywhere else in America, and many of the early stars of the game came from Brooklyn. The tall, lean McCarren became one of the best pitchers in the entire Eastern District. McCarren's favorite team was a club formed in 1855 by a local shipwright named Frank Pidgeon, who had recruited other workers from the Collyer and Webb shipyard in nearby Greenpoint to form a team.

The Eckford players had little time to practice because they worked seventy-hour weeks, but the sawing and hammering involved in their trade made them incredibly fit. McCarren idolized the team's pitcher, Joe Sprague, because that was the position the boy himself played, and many people said of McCarren that the lanky Irish kid was the best young thrower in the Eastern District.

The best team in the newly formed city was a group of well-off young men from South Brooklyn called the Atlantic Club. In 1860, the Eckfords challenged the Atlantics to a three-game series. The Eckfords were intimidated by the awesome reputation of the Atlantics.

Still, the Eckford boys were ahead going into the ninth inning of the first game before the Atlantics pulled it out, scoring four runs in the ninth to win 7-5.

The next week, the Eckford players were even more nervous as they fell behind 9-6 in the fourth inning. Sensing how nervous the team was, Pidgeon addressed the players saying "Now boys, just think that you are playing a common club and forget these fellows are Atlantics." After the speech the boys loosened up and won the second game of the series, 20-15. The Eckfords lost the final game of the series 20-15, but they had established themselves as a serious club that could contend with the top teams.

The war hurt all the Brooklyn baseball teams as young men left their clubs to serve in the Union army. War, however, helped the Eckford Club because it did not lose so many players. When the war broke out in 1861, many baseball teams canceled their seasons. Few games were played that season, but baseball held a season the following year in 1862, and the Eckford club was ready.

The Marions of Williamsburg, their farm team, continued to feed the club excellent young players, including an English-born infielder named Al Reach. He was a wiry man, only about Five-foot-eight tall and weighing one hundred-fifty-five pounds. He quickly made his way into the starting nine of the Eckford team. As a twenty-one-year-old, he rapidly became a star for the Eckford team. He was a good left-handed hitter, but he was no giant. He was known as a "scratcher" for his ability to dig balls out of the dirt. Reach was the first second basemen ever to play off the bag, and his range allowed him to smother balls that would have been hits.

In the 1862 season, Eckford achieved dominance they had never shown before, fueled in part by the diminution of talent other teams suffered. Eckord started the season with an excellent power pitcher, the twenty-four-year-old Joe Sprague. Like many of the young baseball players at the time, though, Sprague felt it was his duty to join the army and fight for his country. He left the team and enlisted for ninety days. Although the team missed Sprague's pitching, they still won without him, and made it to the National championship, which was being held locally at the Union Grounds in Williamsburg.

McCarren and all the other local fans attended all the games of the series, even though they had to pay money to witness the contest. The club now had to win two of the three games against the Atlantics. In the first game of the championship the Eckford club crushed Atlantic 24-14, but Atlantic gained revenge, punishing them in the second match by a ridiculous score of 39-5.

The final game was supposed to be played the following week, but Eckford postponed it for two weeks, stalling for time and hoping to get Sprague back, whose enlistment still had not expired. The team's now numerous new fans clamored for Sprague's return, bombarding the area's congressman, William Wall, with frantic appeals to bring Sprague back to Brooklyn. Wall went to President Lincoln himself to facilitate Sprague's return. Lincoln then ordered General McClellan to release the pitcher, and now Sprague was back to face Atlantic. McCarren and his friends nervously awaited the final deciding game. The ball ground was built on a large block bounded by Harrison Avenue, Rutledge Street and Lynch Street. The grounds were only a year old, and had previously been an outdoor skating rink. No one had ever seen so many spectators, which only added to the excitement of this championship game. Thousands were paying admission and passing through the gates of their new ball field to watch the deciding game between the Eckford Club and their archrivals from South Brooklyn. Thousands more who had not paid were standing outside the wooden fences of the grounds.

Each inning, the huge crowd erupted when

Sprague made his appearance on the mound. The Eckford players became more and more anxious, sensing that they could make history, and finally defeat Atlantic. Sprague's power pitching was awesome, and the Atlantic fans could not believe that the same team that had hit with such power that they scored 39 runs could not hit Sprague's pitches. Batter after batter struck out, and soon Eckford led 9-3. However, the team and its fans were still on edge. They feared that somehow, as before, Atlantic would find a way to win.

As Eckford took the field in the top of the ninth, it seemed that history could be made. No team other than Atlantic had ever won the National Association Championship, but now Eckford was only three outs away. Sprague got two outs quickly. When he struck out the last batter, the Eckford fans became jubilant, with hundreds rushing out onto the field to greet the delirious players. Sprague was mobbed, and for a day Williamsburg forgot the war.

Chapter Ten:
July, 1863

In the summer of 1863, the war was dragging on into its third year. Naïve hopes of a quick victory had proven false. The bodies of some of the men who had gone off to war returned in coffins to Williamsburg. Former Williamsburg Mayor Dr. Clayton Berry had contracted malaria in the swamps of the Virginia during the peninsula campaign. He was brought home, but his health was shattered, and he would be an invalid for the rest of his days. Much of the talk around Williamsburg centered around the Eckford Club, which continued its dominance, winning game after game. There was also much anger about a local garment factory that had been raided by the police, who had discovered that the factory was sewing Rebel uniforms, which were to be smuggled south.

News of the war was bleak. The South was on the offensive. Robert E. Lee and the Army of Northern Virginia had crossed into Pennsylvania, hoping to win a victory on Northern soil, and compel the North to sue for peace. Lee and his Southern army would confront the Union army at a small crossroads town called Gettysburg. One of the New York brigades trying to defeat Lee was the Excelsior brigade commanded by a Tammany Hall politician-turned-General, Dan Sickles.

Williasmburger Sergeant Martin Short was one of the soldiers in Sickles' brigade. In his service in the army Short had proven himself to be a good soldier. He had been captured by the Rebels at Pittsburgh Landing, but was later exchanged in a prisoner swap, rejoining his unit. He won the respect of the men in his unit in a skirmish a few days before Gettysburg when their captain, an Englishman, ironically also called Short, was shot and wounded. Martin Short, seeing Captain Short lying on the ground, ran from cover into a hail of bullets and threw his wounded captain over his large shoulder, then carried him back to safety, gaining him the respect of every soldier in his unit. Short had grown a lot during his two years in the army. He had grown taller, and had become a strong, muscular man with a barrel chest. He was no longer the callow teenager who had enlisted. Everything about him suggested that he was an army sergeant, a rank his heroic action had rightfully earned him.

The 73rd Regiment, with which he served, was now a group of battle-hardened veterans. They knew that they were as brave as their Southern adversaries, but they had continually suffered defeat and many casualties because of bad generalship. They feared a repeat of bad leadership again. On the second day of the battle of Gettysburg, General Sickles, defying a direct order from his commander General Meade, moved his troops forward, occupying higher ground in a peach orchard, but also moving his soldiers out of the range of protective cannon fire, and creating a salient, permitting them to be attacked on two sides. Short and the volunteer firemen in his unit must have grimly thought about the other battles they had been whipped in as they marched forward, full of apprehension. They feared a repeat of the carnage in the battles of Chancellorsville and Fredericksburg, but they were soldiers, and their fate was to follow orders. They correctly sensed that they quickly faced a really tough fight.

Short and the other soldiers, though, could not help but notice the beauty of this Pennsylvania countryside on this sunny summer day. They marched through a wheat field and then were held in reserve at a farm called the Trostle Farm. In the afternoon

Short's regiment found itself still positioned in re-serve to the north of the Trostle Farm lane, support-ing the advanced line along a country lane called the Emmitsburg Road. As the battle rolled toward a near-by peach orchard early that evening, Major Henry Tremain of Sickles' staff (and originally a member in the 73rd) appeared in front of the regiment, coming breathlessly in from the left at a gallop. They knew his message well before he reached them, and quickly the men sprang into line. Facing left, they moved toward the peach orchard at double-quick through a shower of bullets and bursting shells. The 114th Pennsylvania Regiment, stretched along the Emmitsburg road just in front of them, was involved in a fierce fight; men of the 114th were getting hit and falling before Short's eyes.

The 73rd came to a halt on high ground near a farmhouse in the rear of the 114th, which had crossed to the west side of the Emmitsburg Road to engage the enemy, Barksdale's Mississippians. Here Short's unit would have to wait until the 114th had cleared their front, though they were already taking fire from the Mississippians, as shells and bullets whistled in. They did not have to wait long, for soon the 114th began to retreat northward up the road. The 73rd found itself facing waves of the gray-clad 13th and 17th Mississippi, who advanced against them. As the charging Mississippians rose into view above the crest, traversed at that point by the Emmetsburg road, the New York soldiers poured into their faces a hot and ringing volley that felled scores of the Rebels. The Rebels momentarily staggered, but closed up quickly, and with the familiar, "Hi-yi!" returned fire, pressing forward with the savage courage of baited bulls. The Union cannon batteries behind Short were belching shot, shell and grape into the faces of the Southern soldiers' charging columns; showers of branches fell from the peach trees in the orchard in the leaden hurricane that swept Short's regiment from two sides. Every door, window and sash of a nearby house was shivered to atoms. The barn close by was riddled like a sieve from base to roof, and cannon shot at every instant split its boards and timbers into showers of kindling-wood.

Short was aware of the huge amount of lead that was whistling by him, often hitting members of the 73rd who either fell dead or screamed out in pain. The regiment was melting away quickly in the deadly crossfire, but still stood to its work unflinchingly, and the remaining few finally closed in semi-circle around its riddled flag. Their color-bearer was struck dead, but another brave man instantly caught up the flag, waving it defiantly. A bullet shattered his arm in a few minutes, but then a third man held it up again, The men of his company fell dead and wounded beside him, but somehow Colonel Burns, mounted on his conspicuous old white horse, miraculously escaped the bullets. Suddenly, Short felt something slam into his shoulder with tremendous force, and the impact made him drop his rifle. Then, he felt a hot excruciating pain as if he was burned by fire. He had been hit, and he could feel that a hole had been ripped in his shoulder. Soon, warm hot blood started to fill the opening. He lay down writhing in pain, aware that his tunic was filling with blood. The pain was so intense that it was hard to think, but he wondered if the wound in his shoulder would prove fatal. The Southerners charged at Short's regiment, and in the intense firefight there were heavy casualties before Short, and what was left of the regiment, retreated in a hail of bullets.

Short, in great pain, walked to the rear, and he was placed in a wagon with other soldiers, many of whom were wounded far more gravely than he. There were men who had shattered limbs, ghastly head wounds and wounds to the torso. He was still writhing in agony, though he was aware that the blood had stopped flowing out of the wound. As he rode in the wagon and surveyed the rear, he for the first time could see the scale of the carnage. The town of Gettysburg, as well as the fields and woodlands for miles about, was a limitless scene of such horrific carnage and gore. He was brought to a church that had been converted into a field hospital. Hundreds of desperately wounded men were stretched out on boards laid across the high-backed pews as closely as they could be packed together. The tens of thousands of wounded men overwhelmed the surgeons. The heat of the tightly packed, breathless church, the pain from his wound and the horrible stench were almost too much to bear.

Short was one of a hundred and three wounded men from his regiment in the battle. Fifty-one of its soldiers were killed, and the unit suffered a 50% casualty rate. Short was one of the lucky wounded men. The bullet had passed straight through his shoulder. The wound was cauterized, and fortunately it did not develop fatal gangrene. His fight was done now, and he would be heading back to a military hospital in New York.

The local boys in the 47th Regiment were not at Gettysburg. They stayed in the rear and at one moment they were the only unit that guarded the capital. Many of the men were disappointed that they did not see combat, but they would soon see fighting in a place they never could have imagined: the streets of Manhattan.

A few days after the Union won the battle of Gettysburg, a riot over the Drafting of soldiers broke out in Manhattan that became the largest incidence of civil unrest in American history. The spark for the riots was the federal Conscription Act, the nation's first draft, passed by Congress in March 1863. Three years into the Civil War, with desertions, tens of thousands of battlefield deaths and an equal number of deaths from disease, more troops were needed for the Union Army than were being supplied by volunteers. The conscription law targeted men between the ages of twenty and thirty-five and all unmarried white men up to the age of forty-five for military service. Draftees could be released from service by paying $300 (a year's wages for some) to a replacement, ensuring that the draft would target lower-income men. Many white workingmen in New York took this fact as proof of the rumors that once they were drafted, black men would take their jobs.

The first drawing of numbers for the draft in New York City took place on Saturday, July 11 without incident, and over half of the city's two thousand-man quota was drawn. Things changed, however, on Monday the 13th. At 10:00 am, a crowd of at least five hundred men gathered at the Ninth District Provost Marshall's office at Third Avenue and 47th Street, where the draft was taking place. Many members of the crowd were Irish laborers who feared having to compete with emancipated slaves for jobs. They were led by members of Engine Company #33, whose captain had conceived the idea of burning the draft office down to destroy the records so that none of his men would be drafted. The mob attacked the office, throwing paving stones through the windows. It then burst through the front door and set the building ablaze. Another fire company sent to fight the fire was attacked, its horses killed and equipment broken up.

Police superintendent, John A. Kennedy, arrived at the site to check on the situation. Although Kennedy was not in uniform, someone in the mob recognized him, and they attacked him. Kennedy tried to defend himself, but he was left nearly unconscious, having had his face bruised and cut, his eye blackened and his lips swollen; he was beaten to a bloody pulp. Police drew their clubs and revolvers, and charged the crowd, but they were no match for the mob, and quickly anarchy reigned.

The number of rioters grew as the day wore on. A local tavern that refused to serve alcohol was burned. The racist rioters targeted innocent blacks in the streets, many of whom were beaten, tortured and even lynched. One victim was attacked by a crowd of four hundred, beaten with clubs and paving stones, and then hanged and after his corpse was set afire. At least one hundred blacks were murdered in the orgy of killing.

Williamsburgers not only heard reports of the riots from people who returned on the ferry, but they could also see the burning buildings lighting up Manhattan at night. One of the first refugees to reach Williamsburg was a black escapee who swam the East River to escape the riots, Jack Cample. Cample would gain local fame as a cart driver whose distinctive whistling marked his arrival on any street. Other blacks followed him to the area to avoid the pogrom they faced.

Perhaps the most famous refugee to make it across to Williamsburg was Dr. James McCune Smith, the first African American physician in the United States. Barred from studying in America because of his race, Smith went to Glasgow, Scotland where he received a degree in medicine. He set up a black pharmacy and practiced medicine in Manhattan before he and his family fled the riots. He had been the physician to the Colored Children's Orphanage, which was burned by the mob, but thankfully the children were able to escape. Horrified by the riot, he vowed never to return to Manhattan, and set up his new home amongst the black community in Williamsburg.

The anti-slavery Germans of Dutch Town feared that the riots would spread to Williamsburg, and blacks would be murdered. Three hundred armed German men turned out in Williamsburg to protect blacks with at a local sports club, the German Turn Verein. Former Mayor William Wall also pledged $5,000 to buy muskets and ammunition to put down the riots.

Other buildings in the city attacked by the mob included the Mayor's residence, two police stations, and the offices of *The New York Times*. The attack on the *Times* building was stopped by the staff members who fired Gatling guns. The Federal armory at Second Avenue and Twenty-first Street was another target of the rioters. The Mayor desperately telegraphed for troops to put down the riot. The government sent the 47th on a train from Washington to quell the riot.

The Williamsburg soldiers arrived in the city by train on Wednesday, which dawned hot. Many New Yorkers, fearing the city was about to fall to the rioters, spent the day trying to get out of town, clogging the Hudson and East River piers and flooding north out of the city toward the Bronx and Westchester County. The police, many of whom had barely slept in forty-eight hours, tried to keep pace with the rioters. The 47th's presence on the streets, along with the presence of several thousand other soldiers, convinced many rioters to end their looting. The 47th shot some of the remaining looters, but its presence, along with other combat troops rushed into the city, signaled the end of the riots.

The riots re-enforced in the minds of the soldiers in the 47th the difference between the traitors in Manhattan and the loyal union supporters back home in Brooklyn. When they learned of the scale of the murder and destruction, the men of the 47th were proud they had played a part in crushing it. They were heroes, but another local hero would win a medal of honor in battle, and gain even more fame for his fighting without a gun.

Chapter Eleven:
The War Finally Ends

Throughout the war's first two years, the newly erected Havemeyer plant on the waterfront continued to refine sugar and rake in huge wartime profits. The original partners, however, could not see eye-to-eye on expansion and they split. Fredrick Havemeyer, looking to grow his business and requiring a lot of capital, invited his brother-in-law, rich merchant James Elder, to join the firm. Havemeyer used the money Elder invested to help Theodore expand the plant, which soon covered the entire blocks of South Second Street, South Third Street, and most of the block from South Fourth Street to South Fifth Street.

Even though its supply of Louisiana sugar had been cut off, the refinery still turned out tons of sugar. The Havemeyers replaced the lost American sugar with Cuban sugar as foreign-flagged vessels each day laden with a million pounds of imported raw Cuban sugar docked at the Havemeyer pier, and unloaded their cargoes of huge wooden casks of raw sugar, as Irish longshoremen carted it a few steps into the refinery. The Refinery worked seven days a week, twenty-four hours a day, churning out white refined sugar, and the pungent odor of sugar became a regular scent along the Williamsburg waterfront.

The war was a godsend for sugar refiners, as the scarcity of sugar drove up the price and huge, un-imagined profits rolled into Havemeyer and Elder. The government of the United States proved to be the best customer the Havemeyers had. Each soldier in the Union army got a rations of fifteen pounds of sugar a month, far more than the two to three pounds the average person consumed in a month. Prices tripled, and Havemeyer and Elder recorded record profits.

Even during the war, sugar refining was chang-ing and becoming even more industrial. In 1863, the Havemeyers realized that they had to abandoned the cumbersome, outdated mold system of forming sugar loaves in favor of the centrifuge that was an innova-tion of a competitor, Jersey City's F.O. Matthieson. The centrifuge Matthieson employed was a large, perforat-ed basket spinning very rapidly, much like a washing machine in the spin cycle, which spun and dried the sugar mixture, yielding golden raw sugar in a much shorter time period than with the mold system.

Though Theodore Havemeyer was working long hours in the refinery, he still found time to court one of the most-eligible young women in Manhattan, Ms. Emile de Loosy, the daughter of the Austrian Consul to New York and a Catholic. They soon married, and Havemeyer promised to raise the children from the marriage as Catholics. His wife would bear Theodore nine children. Through his Catholic wife, Havemeyer became friendly with Father Malone of the Saints Peter and Paul church, and the Havemeyers often visited Father Malone's church to hear his sermons, many of which were political in nature, praising the righteousness of the Union cause. Taking a stance few Irish-American priests took at the time, Malone courageously spoke out against the Draft Riots, and condemned the orgy of hate that led to lynching of African-Americans. Father Malone soon became the confessor of Mrs. Havemeyer and became a lifelong friend of Theodore Havemeyer. They gave him large sums of money, which some of his parishioners commented upon. The gifts from the Havemeyers perhaps had an effect, for Malone never said a word against them or their management of the refinery where so many of his flock worked.

After the death of his son George in front of his

eyes, a crushed Fredrick Havemeyer passed more and more control of his plant to his son Theodore. Aged fifty-four, Fredrick had grown tired of the stress of running the refinery, and he wanted to live the life of a country gentlemen. He sold the Manhattan mansion he had inherited from his father and purchased a sixty-acre parcel on the East River at Throgg's Neck with a spectacular view of Manhattan, where he built a three-story colonnaded house with a mansard roof, huge porch and a boat dock, which he called Beau Rivage. He had a formal garden planted around the house, and invited his large family there to weekend with him. However, the death of one of his children would haunt him again. In 1865, his favorite daughter Mary died. She had consoled him when his wife had passed and had acted as a mother to his younger children, left a boarding school to take care of them. Fredrick was inconsolable.

In 1864, the war dragged into its fourth year, but victory proved elusive. At the start of the war, Willis Hodges seemed to disappear from his church and questions about his whereabouts remained unanswered. On January 1, 1863 finally, Hodges' many years of prayers were answered when President Lincoln issued the Emancipation Proclamation. Though he was too old to fight, Hodges would help to redress the wrongs done to his mother and his people by traveling to Virginia and working as a guide and spy for the union army, while helping slaves to escape to freedom.

In 1864, Williamsburg was thrilled by reports that one of their own, Sergeant Walter Jamieson, had won the Congressional Medal of Honor. Jamieson was born in France to Scottish parents who moved to Brooklyn when he was thirteen years old. Apprenticed as a machinist, Sam, as Jamieson was also known, was a small but powerfully built, thickset young man with a large protruding nose. As a boy, he excelled at swimming and boxing, fighting and winning his first bare-knuckled boxing match at nineteen in 1859.

When the war broke out Jamieson enlisted in the 129th Regiment. He soon proved to be absolutely calm and level-headed in combat, rising in rank from corporal to sergeant on the basis of his courage in battle. On September 29, 1864, his regiment was attacking Fort Harrison. They ran forward at a dead run through a torrent of grapeshot that killed many in his unit, including fellow Williamsburger Tom Dane, a champion rower. They finally reached a hill that shielded them from the withering fire and regrouped for the final assault on the fort. One of the officers handed the regimental flag to Jamieson, saying that he was the man who would plant it on the top of the fort's walls, but also making him a marked man, since the Rebels always concentrated their fire on the flag-bearer. His unit charged over the hill again into a withering fire. Jamieson reached the base of the fort's walls, and asked to be boosted up so that he could mount the walls. A fellow WIlliamsburger, George Wolff, followed him, clambering up onto the wall and hoisting up the regimental flag on the ramparts. When the Rebels inside the fort saw Jamieson and Wolff with the flag, they mistakenly assumed that the whole regiment was coming in from behind them, and a large number surrendered. Jamieson received the Medal of Honor for his bravery in this skirmish, but the battle would not be the last fight by far that he would see.

When Lee surrendered at Appomattox the bells of all the Williamsburg churches peeled, but the joy would be cut short just a few days later by the murder of Abraham Lincoln. No one felt more grief than Father Malone, who preached perhaps his finest sermon ever, emotionally proclaiming from the pulpit that Lincoln was a martyr and confronting those in his congregation who approved of his assassination:

> I ask you to mark well the man calling himself a
> Catholic, who shall dare to speak approvingly of his

assassination, lest he bring disgrace on us all. Pray that the life and integrity of the nation be preserved. Pray that the constituted authority of the nation may pass through this trying ordeal unharmed, and that this rebellion may speedily be destroyed.

He commented specifically on Lincoln's murder, saying:

It is not that Abraham Lincoln has been murdered. It is more. It is the President of the United States, the representative of a nation of free men, the head and chosen of the people. We mourn this day for this Christian patriot gone from us, but we stand appalled and horror stricken at the murder of the magistrate whose heart so filled with Christian charity and forgiveness for those who had forgotten their allegiance, taken their arms against the most humane government on earth.

The end of the war would usher in a new age in American history when big business would grow so rich and dominant that it threatened to dwarf the democratic institutions that the Constitution creat-ed. Amongst the richest members of this new class of millionaires were the Havemeyers, and in the eyes of many they would come to represent all that was wrong with emerging industrial capitalism. They would make Williamsburg the center of the empire they would create.

Chapter Twelve:
Apprenticeships

While many Americans were dying or suffering grievous wounds on the battlefield, others were becoming rich and transforming America into a modern capitalist and corporate society. A new class of millionaires arose during the Civil War by fulfilling large government contracts, but often with cheap, substandard or even defective goods. The new dishonest businessmen who became rich during the Civil War were called, "shoddy millionaires." Mark Twain coined the term that perfectly described the new post-war age, calling the epoch: "the Gilded Age."

New York became home to these new "shoddy millionaires" and emerged even more clearly as the country's financial center. New York bankers became rich when an 1864 Federal Banking Act invested all federal funds in New York City. The value of real estate doubled in the city between 1860 and 1870. By 1869, the

New York Stock Exchange was trading $3,000,000,000 in securities. In the same year corrupt financiers Jay Gould and Jim Fisk almost succeeded in cornering the gold market thanks to the assistance of President Grant's brother-in-law who convinced the president to keep federal gold out of the market, driving up the price. The corrupt financiers made a killing by dumping their inflated gold holdings right before the market plummeted because the Federal government finally began to sell gold.

The corrosive power of money appeared not only on Wall Street, but also even on McCarren's beloved Eckford baseball team. By 1864, money was transforming baseball from an amateur sport played for love of the game to a sport ruled by money. Eckford Club founder Frank Pidgeon had always warned about the destructive power of money in sport, and now he and young McCarren were seeing greed destroy the club. The gentlemanly traditions that were part of the sport at its founding were disappearing. In 1864, Eckford's rivals the Atlantic club, angry over their loss of the baseball crown, refused to give the Eckford Club the customary pre-game cheer, or to participate in the post-game social, which had always been a part of the game's civility. Frank Pidgeon, the Eckford Club's founder, saw so many signs of ungentlemanly behavior in the game he loved that he left in disgust before the start of the 1864 season.

The Atlantics and other clubs were doing something that was even more in violation of the league rules Pidgeon had established - they were paying money under the table. Players began mysteriously to jump from one team to the next. Joe Sprague, the Eckford Club star pitcher, jumped to Atlantic, though surprisingly he played shortstop not pitcher, for them.

It was no secret that talented infielder Al Reach wanted to follow in Sprague's path. He was openly courting the owner of the Philadelphia Athletics, Patrick Fitzgerald, to pay him to join his club. Other Eckford members showed ungentlemanly behavior in other ways. Waddy Beach, the star catcher, was so badly hurt in a barroom brawl that he was unable to play the 1864 season.

The Eckford club had capable replacements, but it was more than the loss of some of the team stars that seemed to be affecting the club. A malaise seemed to spread throughout the club, and Henry Chadwick, the astute Brooklyn baseball journalist, noted the change in spirit in the club after they lost to the Brooklyn Eagles: "We could scarcely realize that it was the same club that had gone through the last season in such brilliant style." Chadwick noted in his report that the team desperately missed Pidgeon's enthusiasm.

The next year, 1865, things went from bad to worse for Eckford. Al Reach left for Philadelphia and made history. He became the first openly professional baseball player with Fitzgerald paying him a salary of $25 a week. Outfielder Jimmy Wood left for Chicago. William Wansley, Tommy Devyr and shortstop Ed Duffy also left The Eckford Club for the Mutuals. However, there were other more scandalous events that would prove Pidgeon's fears well founded.

1865 would end with an incident that Pidgeon had predicted when he established the amateur-only rule. In September, gambler Kane McLaughlin paid William Wansley, Tom Devyr and Ed Duffy of the New York Mutuals 100$ each to throw a game they were playing against their former team, the Eckfords the following day. By all accounts it looked like a normal game until the fifth inning, when the Mutuals allowed eleven runs through "over-pitched balls, wild throws, passed balls, and failures to stop them in the field." The crowd, growing angry at the obvious fix, shouted out that the game was rigged. Later, all three admitted their role in the scandal, and were banned from baseball. The lesson of the incident was, however, clear to many: the only way to keep game-fixing out of the sport was to pay the players enough money for them to refuse bribes.

Pat McCarren had grown into a young man of great personal ambition, despite his humble background. He had witnessed fortunes being made around him, and he also wanted to become rich. Too poor to continue his education, McCarren had to find a trade. He could have apprenticed with his father as a carpenter, but being a perceptive young man, he realized that coopers, who made the barrels the sugar and oil industry consumed in huge numbers, would be very much in demand, so in 1865, he made the wise choice of becoming an apprentice cooper.

Sugar was not the only major local refining industry requiring barrels; North Brooklyn was also the nation's center for oil refining. Bushwick Inlet on the southern edge of Williamsburg became the first place large-scale oil refining was done in the United States, and for decades no place on earth refined more oil than North Brooklyn. Charles Pratt became a millionaire and the richest man in Brooklyn by setting up the Astral Oil works on the banks of Bushwick Inlet in 1867. His refinery became the nation's first modern refinery, capable of producing tens of thousands of gallons of kerosene and other oils, all of which were shipped in wooden barrels. Other refiners soon followed Pratt to North Brooklyn, with more than fifty refineries eventually lining the East River from Williamsburg to Greenpoint.

The local sugar industry, with its huge need for barrels, was also growing very quickly. After the Civil War, there was a scarcity of raw sugar, driving prices up. Prices for sugar were 285% higher in 1865 than in 1860, so firms producing sugar were very profitable. Capital rushed into sugar production, increasing output and competition. Demand was rapidly increasing across the nation as mechanization had created uniformly high-quality, low-cost sugar that could be produced in mass quantities. Sugar was also reaching the tables of millions of Americans thanks to the railroad. Sugar became a staple product that was dependent on the production of huge numbers of barrels made by local coopers.

The post-Civil War years were a boom time for sugar, especially in North Brooklyn. By 1870, Sugar refining had become Brooklyn's most important industry, and it had transformed the Williamsburg waterfront. A mile and a half of Williamsburg waterfront had seven large refineries, each with a huge need for coopers to make barrels for its growing business. From 1869 to 1874, three to four new firms entered the market every year. Williamsburg had emerged as the capital of American sugar refining, which employed hundreds of coopers.

Years later, Patrick McCarren recalled that the happiest day of his life was the day that he became a journeyman cooper after suffering three years of hell as an apprentice. In the days after the Civil War when McCarren was learning his trade, it was common practice to abuse apprentices physically when they made mistakes. McCarren was hit hard with a slap if a barrel leaked. After many slaps, punches and words of insult, McCarren learned the art of tapering the staves that comprise the barrel with an axe. He mastered the technique of hollowing each stave out with a knife and rounding the outside corners. McCarren also learned how to joint the barrel so that it did not leak, because a journeyman cooper never used anything to caulk or glue the barrel. He learned how to mount the staves in an iron raising hoop, and to soften the wood by lighting a small fire, then drive the hoops into place so that the barrel was watertight, and to cut grooves into the top so that the head of the cask would fit properly. McCarren mastered the craft so perfectly that he needed no instruments to measure the wood pieces that formed the barrel. He had developed an eye as accurate as any ruler. He had learned not only how to make barrels that were watertight, but also how to make them quickly enough so that he could keep pace with any journeyman cooper. At age nineteen, he could proudly and confidently call himself a craftsman.

Not far away, another young man had apprenticed himself to a trade learning the sugar business, and that young man would serve a five-year apprenticeship, mastering the details of every job in the plant and every machine in the large refinery. The young man was Henry O. Havemeyer, the most rebellious and talented scion of the family. He was born into the famous sugar family in 1847, the eighth of ten children. Henry was named after the brother-in-law of his father, Dr. Henry Senff, the family physician, but he was called Harry as he grew up. Harry grew up in luxury in a brownstone on Fourteenth Street. From a young age, his older brother Thomas, who was also destined to enter the family firm, was his inseparable companion. When he was just four years old, his mother died after a lingering illness. It is hard to speculate what effect the passing of his mother had on Harry, but it robbed him of a mother's love, and probably made him sterner and more self-reliant.

After Harry's mother's passing, his sister Mary left boarding school to raise her two younger brothers, and Mary became the closest thing to a mother Harry ever had. At age seven, Harry was sent off to boarding schools, where he proved to be a pugnacious and defiant student who often got into fistfights with the other boys. His temper was so volatile that he could no longer stay in school because of his fisticuffs. At age twelve, after believing that he was unfairly reprimanded because of a fistfight with another boy, he asked to come home to Fourteenth Street, ending his schooling for good. He began commuting to Williamsburg by ferry, quickly learning every aspect of the family business. Years later, he would proudly tell people that he had grown up in a sugar refinery.

When he was just Eighteen his sister Mary, who had been more of a mother than a sister, passed away, leaving Harry to grieve again. The same year, Harry and his brother Thomas became apprenticed to Joseph Elder, Mary's husband, who taught the boys every aspect of the commercial side of the business. Harry proved to be a quick study, far more suited to mastering the intricacies of sales, costs and pricing than his older brother Thomas. He quickly mastered all that his brother-in law could teach him, and he seemed to have an innate feel for the sugar market that was well beyond his years. He also showed himself to be highly self-disciplined, with a keen work ethic and a burning desire to succeed. If he pushed himself hard, then he pushed those under him equally hard, demanding a high level of work from them, and unleashing his volcanic temper on subordinates when they did not meet his demands. He had a sharp eye for buying and selling the product, and perhaps no one in America was more adept at reading the fluctuations in the sugar market and predicting its movements. Quickly, everyone in the family firm realized that of the three brothers, Harry was born to manage a business, and after his brother George's death, he was more and more regarded as the one destined to run the company when Fredrick retired.

In 1867, Harry and his brother Thomas made their first grand tour of Europe. Harry and Thomas visited London, Paris, Geneva, Rome, Florence and Naples. It was Harry's first real exposure to European art, an experience which not only deeply affected Harry, but would also leave a lasting affect on American art collecting. Harry's appetite for Rembrandt was first whetted when he saw the Dutchman's works in the Louvre. Although Harry could be abrasive and aggressive, he also possessed a strong aesthetic sense, and he would become not only a great art collector, but also even an accomplished, self-taught violin player who sometimes played with professional musicians.

Quickly, no one doubted that Harry, aged only twenty-one, was the heir-apparent to succeed Elder in sugar marketing. He was made a partner in the firm, and it would soon be clear to all that he was the man to run it. Harry was imperious, abrasive and domineering, but he also exhibited all the traits of a leader. Just having reached manhood, Harry was showing that by force of personality he would soon become the dominant person in the Havemeyer family, and he would be anointed by his father as "the Sugar King." In an 1874 letter, Fredrick put into words what was clear already to most by 1868: "Get it down as a fact that Harry is the king of the sugar market."

In 1868, he again experienced the shock of death when Joseph Elder died at the young age of thirty-six. Once more, Harry was devastated because he had grown close to his brother-in-law who had mentored him in running the commercial side of the business. The Elders had been lifelong friends of his father, and Harry had known Joseph's niece Louise from childhood. Soon a romance blossomed between Louise, who was twenty-three, and Harry, who was two years younger.

Chapter Thirteen:
Love and Wars - 1867

After being mustered out of his regiment at the end of the Civil War, Walter Jamieson ended up in Baltimore with a group of men who promoted him as a bare-knuckled boxer called Sam Collyer. Jamieson continued to fight, but the engagements he now fought in were no longer on the battlefield, but in secretly staged boxing matches. Collyer had become a hero in Williamsburg, idolized not just for his bravery in battle, but even more for his valor in the ring.

Because boxing was illegal, they had ended up outside in this remote field in the bitter cold of January, when no one wanted to be outside, even if he had to. Eight hundred paying spectators from New York, Philadelphia, Baltimore and Washington, whom *The New York Times* described as "principally roughs, fighters and thieves," had braved the snow and the intense cold of this January morning to come to a potato field eighteen miles from the Goldsboro, Pennsylvania train depot to witness the bout for the lightweight championship of America.

After a heavy snowstorm, the promoters had somehow not only pitched a twenty-four foot-square ring, but also cleared the snow from around it. They had erected an outer ring for the journalists there to report on the fight, and the two physicians who would treat the wounds the fighters received. The two fighters fought without gloves under the "London Rules," which allowed a combatant to grab his opponent and throw him to the ground, as well as to hit him with his bare fists. A round ended when one of the fighters fell, or took a knee.

Although he was the smaller fighter, Collyer was the favorite to win the bout. He weighed perhaps a hundred-fifteen or a hundred-twenty pounds at most, and stood only five-foot-five and a half, but he was extremely tough; he was not only able to give a beating with his fast fists, but more importantly he was able to take the brutal beatings that were part of the sport. He had whipped three good fighters in bare-knuckled matches the previous year, first beating Mike Carr in Baltimore in March in only fourteen rounds. Then, in April, he beat Horatio Bolster in forty-seven rounds in Alexandria, Virginia, but his most impressive win came against "Young" Barney Aaron" outside a small Virginia town. A fighter whom many pugilists were afraid to box for years, ten years earlier Aaron had won the lightweight title, becoming the first Jewish boxer to win an American title. The war, however, had stopped his career. Aaron and Collyer fought a bout legendary for the punishment each boxer withstood. The fight went forty-seven rounds, and lasted a grueling two hours and five minutes. Although Collyer won, both he and Aaron were bloody pulps who had to be carried out of the ring on stretchers.

Collyer entered the freezing ring to cheers, and stripped down. McGlade leapt over the ropes with a smile that would soon be wiped from his face. He not only outweighed the ex-solider, but looked much more muscular. Collyer appeared serious and preoccupied before the bell. It was bitterly cold, but soon the two fighters were no longer aware of the intense cold, so focused were they on the fight. In the first three rounds Collyer landed some hard rights on McGlade, who tried to inflict damage on Collyer's ribs. Collyer knocked him down once, and knocked him flying back to his corner twice. The smile that had been on Mc-Glade's face before the bout vanished with the first knockdown, and did not return. In the fifth round, Collyer connected with a fearsome blow that elicited cries from the spectators of, "Kill him Sam," and "Cut the heart out of him." During the next six or seven rounds, Collyer continued to inflict much more damage, landing so many blows that McGlade went down to a knee a few times to avoid more punishment.

In the thirteenth round, Collyer got McGlade into the corner, and inflicted a severe beating. The crowd, sensing a knockout, cried out "Break his neck on the ropes," and, "Kill the son of a bitch." McGlade continued to fight on, though it was clear he was getting beaten badly by Collyer.

Collyer continued to be the aggressor throughout the next dozen rounds, but suddenly, in the thirty-sixth round, McGlade seemed to catch a second wind, and stunned Collyer with a shot that knocked Collyer down, much to the delight of the cheering McGlade supporters. Over the next few rounds, McGlade had the upper hand, and many sensed the fight had shifted in his favor.

In the forty-first round, Collyer revived, and again gained the upper hand, administering a number of blows to McGlade's body. In the forty-fifth round, Collyer wrestled McGlade to the ground, falling heavily on him. Entering the ring, McGlade's partisans claimed that Collyer had fouled him. Collyer's partisans also entered the ring, and suddenly knives and pistols were drawn. A melee in the ring ensued between both sets of partisans, punches flew and some toughs tried to stab their enemies. The frightened journalists moved away from the ring, rightfully afraid of being shot or stabbed. One McGlade supporter was pistol-whipped by a Collyer fan, just outside the ring.

The ring, though, was somehow miraculously cleared, and the fight re-commenced. Collyer hit his opponent with a tremendous shot in the forty-sixth that staggered McGlade. Sensing victory, Collyer did not go back to his corner, but stayed in the ring, awaiting McGlade's entrance in the next round. Collyer again knocked McGlade down, and the bigger man had trouble rising to his feet. The referee called the fight, declaring Collyer the victor to the delight of the his fans. The fight was over in just an hour.

Collyer and McGlade were arrested by the police later that evening, but Collyer later returned to Williamsburg a champion and a hero. Cashing in on his fame, Collyer opened a bar on Siegel Street. He would continue fighting, but years later he would suffer a humiliating loss to another Williamsburg lightweight who would turn out to be one of the greatest fighters who ever put on a pair of gloves.

While Collyer was fighting for a prize far from Williamsburg, Lowell Palmer was battling for a much more lucrative prize right along the East River shoreline. Palmer hoped to become the local barrel and transport business king, the control of which would make him a millionaire many times over. He would achieve success and wealth beyond his wildest dreams.

In 1867, aged just twenty-two, Lowell Palmer arrived in Brooklyn. The Ohio- born son of a Presbyterian minister, Palmer was enrolled as a sixteen-year-old student in Case Western University when Fort Sumter was attacked. Palmer responded to Lincoln's call for volunteers and became a soldier in the artillery, serving in all the battles that the Army of the Cumberland fought in Tennessee and Georgia for the Union. His bravery and ability helped him to rise to the rank of Captain, and he became a member of General Schofield's staff.

At the end of the war, he came to Brooklyn to work for an uncle who was a prominent leather merchant. At twenty-two, he proved so adept at management that he was put in charge of all of his uncle's warehouses. Palmer, like Patrick McCarren, realized that there was a fortune to be made in the production of barrels for Williamsburg's many refineries. He left the leather business, and opened his own cooperage, soon establishing himself as the leading barrel producer in Williamsburg.

In 1870, he noticed that the local sugar refiners had a costly problem with transporting their refined sugar to railheads to be shipped nationally. He suggested to the Erie Railroad that he build a tugboat and a lighter, or transport barge, to ship in the wood and other materials he needed for his barrel-making business. Three years later, Palmer purchased a car float and a tugboat to transport freight cars to and from the Williamsburg location. A car float was an unpowered barge, towed by a tugboat, with rail tracks mounted on its deck that could be used to move railroad cars across the East River.

The freight cars were loaded aboard the car float, and picked up at the Erie facility in New Jersey where other cars were also picked up. Then, they were brought back to Williamsburg to be unloaded along the bulkhead at the water's edge. Palmer soon astutely realized that Havemeyer and Elder would also benefit from having a fleet of such ships to haul their massive refined sugar cargoes across the harbor. In that same year, he established a terminus for the Erie railroad at the foot of North Fifth Street with the great sugar refinery as his main, extremely lucrative, customer. The terminus, called Palmer's Dock, very quickly had far more freight than he could ever have imagined, posing huge logistical problems that he was eventually able to solve. The Board of Aldermen granted permission for trains to cross Kent at North Fifth Street, where he erected a brick depot three-stories high extending to Wythe Avenue. Palmer would soon become the boss of one of the busiest rail yards in all America.

In 1874, the Havemeyers realized that Palmer was a transport and logistics genius, so they turned over their entire cooperage business to the twenty-nine-year old wizard, and they also became co-partners in Palmer's Dock. They organized a new company to manage their massive barrel business called the Brooklyn Cooperage Company, placing Palmer at its head as president. Quickly, Palmer's new company helped Havemeyer and Elder increase its profitability by cutting its labor, storage and transport costs. Palmer soon acquired more waterfront real estate, and laid out a rail yard that had twenty rail lines where six hundred freight cars could be sided. The terminal he constructed could soon handle two hundred fifty freight cars a day, but space was still at a premium. Palmer ingeniously conceived of storing the massive amounts of coal needed by the sugar refineries above the yard, and he built the first elevated coal pockets in American history there. In the first year, only the Erie railroad operated in his terminal, but the market there was so huge and lucrative that soon other railroads vied to lease space from Palmer in the terminal.

Palmer had another brilliant idea. In 1874, he built Brooklyn's first float bridge to facilitate moving freight cars from the East River to his terminal. A float bridge is basically a bridge span anchored to land on one end, running out into the water over pontoons, which support the bridge in the water. Over time, three other float bridges would be built, so that a huge amount of water-borne freight traffic could be handled at his dock.

The partnership with Palmer was the first time that Havemeyer and Elder had offered a controlling interest in the business to someone who was not a member of the family. Allowing Palmer into the business was a wise and very profitable decision for the Havemeyers. For years, Palmer proved to be a brilliant partner who would serve as a director in the family business. Later, he would even help them set up a revolutionary business organization.

In 1870, the twenty-two-year-old Harry married Louise Elder, two years his senior, preserving a family tradition of marrying into the families of business partners. He had grown up with his bride, and was extremely close to her family, regarding her uncle as a mentor, but the marriage would prove to be rocky almost from the outset. The couple embarked on a four-month-long grand tour of Europe, in which Harry hoped to show his new wife the European paintings he loved so much. While he was away, his brother Thomas was left to run the marketing and sales end of the business.

Patrick McCarren was too ambitious to remain a cooper. By 1873, McCarren had left his job in the cooperage, finding work with the government as a barrel inspector. While working as an inspector, he met two oil refiners who would later employ his legislative talents in Albany. Perhaps they suggested to the ambitious young Irish-American that he would be financially rewarded for protecting the oil industry in the capital. The first of the men he met was John D. Rockefeller, who had started his Standard Oil Company in Cleveland, Ohio, but was now intent on dominating the New York oil refining market by buying up Brooklyn refineries like the Astral Oil Company, located on Bushwick Creek in Williamsburg. The following year, Rockefeller would convince the manager of the Astral Oil Company to merge with Standard, forming a corporate trust that would serve as model for Harry Havemeyer's reorganization of the sugar industry. As a barrel inspector, McCarren must have been keenly aware of the massive profits the Williamsburg oil refiners were earning. Perhaps someone also convinced the ambitious young inspector not to report some of the numerous violations he must have observed in the sometimes-leaky barrels.

It is little surprise that the ambitious McCarren should marry above his station. In 1873, he courted and married a teacher, Janet Hogan, much against the wishes of her father, who looked down on the uneducated barrel inspector. McCarren strove to educate himself, and one of the attractions in the match must have been the fact that Hogan was not only an attractive young woman, but also an intelligent and educated woman, who could help McCarren to improve his speech and sound more like an eloquent elected official. McCarren was eager to find a woman who was intelligent enough help him become a polished orator, capable of making the kind of speeches that get politicians elected. A strong love developed quickly between McCarren and his wife. She would bear him five children, but tragically, she and all their children would die young, haunting McCarren until the end of his days.

McCarren's childhood baseball team, the Eckford Club, became a local harbinger of the changing America. The once-proud amateur Eckford team was losing many of its games, as baseball transitioned from an amateur game to a professional sport. One of its stars, outfielder Jimmy Wood, lured by a paycheck, left to play for the newly formed Chicago White Sox in 1870. Eckford tried to make it as a semi-professional team, but also lost many of its other star players to professional teams. Perhaps the unkindest cut of all happened when Wood, who had become a player manager in Chicago, returned, and raided Eckford of its last stars. The formerly mighty Eckfords could not compete with paid players, and the team finally folded in 1872. Perhaps no other place in America than Williamsburg would be more affected by the changes that were transforming America after the Civil War. Soon the bucolic town of church spires on the Banks of the East River would be unrecognizable, as industrialization on a massive scale blighted the once beautiful area.

Chapter Fourteen:
Collections - 1876

Captain Martin Short of the Brooklyn Police Department had soon become a familiar and beloved figure in the Fourteenth Ward. As the powerful captain walked through the streets with his slow, lordly gait, he collected the greetings and bows of the many locals who adored the soft-spoken Irish cop. For those with a long memory, it was ironic that he was one of those Irish immigrants who thirty years ago the Nativists wanted to drive out of the neighborhood. Now, Short was part of the establishment, the embodiment of local law and order. A nine- year veteran of the department, Short had grown into a gentle giant, quiet in manner, yet large and strong enough to be able to handle any criminal. Beloved by the poor of Williamsburg for his generosity, Short summed up his role in the community, saying, "Every good citizen is my friend; every bad one is my enemy."

Short had returned to Williamsburg after the war, and had apprenticed himself to an axle maker on Driggs Avenue and North Fourth Street. Economic depression made life hard during the winter of 1867, and Short's employer had little work. One day during that winter, Short met Republican District Leader Sam Maddox, who admired the war veteran, having heard about his heroism during the war. Although Short was a Democrat, Maddox believed that Short would make a fine cop, and he offered to help the Irishman join the force.

Maddox needed to have tough, honest lawmen like Short join the force. The Brooklyn Police Department after the Civil War was in complete disarray, and crime was rampant. Albany lawmakers, not local politicians, controlled the department, so local citizens had little control over their local police, who largely ignored the residents' needs. Adding insult to injury, despite their inability to tackle crime, the cost of policing Brooklyn had risen 400% in the eight years between 1857 and 1865, a burden to the local taxpayers. Short readily accepted Maddox's offer, joining the Brooklyn Police Department and serving two years in other parts of Brooklyn before being assigned to the Eastern District.

Short quickly proved to be the answer to the long-suffering citizens' prayers and the crooks' nightmares.

Men collect different things, but short had a black bound account book in which he collected the names of the criminals he arrested and the lengths of their sentences. The long list of nabbed crooks in the book proved Short's excellence as a crime fighter, though Short did not look like a detective at all. Short often half closed his eyes in a dopey manner. Seemingly, he was not paying attention, but his dopey appearance hid an astuteness, which helped him to solve many crimes. In 1870, a gang of burglars had infested the Sixth Ward, robbing residents who implored the police to nab the thieves. Captain Mullen detailed Short to hunt down and break up the gang. Two weeks, later Short broke the case when he led a posse of officers to the gang's lair on Meeker and Graham. They arrested a dozen thieves, finding burglar tools and a huge stash of loot.

The arrests led to Short's promotion to Detective Sergeant, and led to his permanent transfer to Williamsburg, which was suffering from a rash of robberies. Short, with his shrewdness and common sense, made a great detective. Soon, he had many of the crooks behind bars. Short broke up the North Sixth and Seven Street Gangs who were skilled burglars. Short also nabbed the members of the Silva Gang, who had often choked and robbed their victims. He then hunted down the Hart Gang, who lived in the area, but robbed in Queens, with Joe Hart, the gang leader, getting a twenty-five year-sentence.

He broke up other gangs as well. In 1873, he broke up a ring of street thieves by watching local pawnshops and tracing the goods pawned there to the thieves. Short was so good at breaking up gangs that notorious Skinny Wilson and the Meeker Avenue Gang left the precinct in fear. He had one close call, though, that nearly cost him his life. Short was nearly shot and killed the next year while arresting members of the Cart Gang. Short had just nabbed three crooks, and he turned one of the robbers over to a fellow officer. The suspect being turned over broke free from Short's colleague and drew a revolver, which he aimed at Short. Short's colleague reacted just in time to knock the criminal's arm forward, and the shot flew above Short's head. Short then tackled the gun-wielding robber, but it was one of the very few times Short had any problem arresting a crook. Most of the time, when the criminals saw the barrel chested Short, they surrendered without resistance. Short was so good at his work, and so loved by the people of the Eastern District, that he even won a competition held by a New York paper for the most popular cop in the United States. Short collected 100,000 votes, winning the competition by a wide margin, and receiving a paid-up life insurance policy as the prize.

Henry Havemeyer and Louise Elder's marriage was in its sixth year in 1876, but it was far from happy. Havemeyer had already developed a balding head and a bulging belly, with blue eyes that were compared to searchlights for their intensity. Louise had grown afraid of her husband's fierce temper. Harry often flew into rages that frightened her. He drank very heavily, and he was often moody and irritable. Her attempts to calm his wrath only seemed to make him more irate. Louise became increasingly unstable, and she often suffered bouts of depression. He seemed never to have a free moment, and he quickly grew into a taciturn man of few words with her.

She had learned to keep her distance from him because he needed solitude and time to think. When interrupted he could become abrupt and severe. To relieve the huge stress that came from running his part of the huge company, he often played the violin, or worse, descended into bouts of drunkenness. He was brusque and overbearing, yet at times he could also still be charming and genteel. The couple could feel a widening divide growing between them.

Havemeyer had thrown himself into his work since becoming a partner and head of merchandising, especially after his father officially retired from the firm in 1872. Harry was emerging as the dominant partner, far more driven than his more easy-going brother Theodore. Harry pushed his subordinates as hard as he pushed himself, and he often placed his employees in open competition with each other to test their strength and resolve. When they failed to meet his lofty expectations he often wrote them scathing letters. The 1870s were a time of increasing competition as more and more firms entered the refinery business, increasing supply and cutting both the price of wholesale sugar and the profit margin. Firms were being driven to the wall by the cutthroat competition of the marketplace, and Harry was determined he and his company would emerge as the victors. He would take the railroad down from his mansion in Stamford, Connecticut, arriving at the company's Wall Street Office and often staying late into the evening.

The strain of the job was not only affecting Harry, but it was also affecting Thomas, his far more sensitive brother, who was increasingly hiding from the stress of the job by going into day-long drinking binges, which sent Henry into a fury. Harry confronted his brother, demanding that he confess his drinking binges to their father, while asking the old man's forgiveness. Complicating Thomas' situation was his love for a woman that the family considered to be beneath their pedigree. Thomas' refusal to break with her only deepened his gloom and isolated him from his brothers. His drinking problem soon drove him out of the family business.

Although the marriage was proving rocky, Harry was still on excellent terms with his in-laws. He was shocked when his childhood friend, Louise's brother George, died in 1873, aged only forty-two years. George was buried in Green-Wood Cemetery with the Havemeyer family in a mausoleum constructed by Harry's father Fredrick. Harry became executor of the will, comforting George's widow, while also comforting George's eighteen-year-old daughter Louisine, his wife's niece. Perhaps it was during this period that he first conceived an attraction for the young woman who would later grow into the love of his life, becoming his second wife.

Harry needed an escape from the huge pressure of running the refinery, and he found great solace in collecting art. Although Harry had all the ferocity of a lion, he also had honed a highly developed aesthetic sense. He fell in love with the French Barbizon School of painting, and made his first acquisition of a Barbizon canvas in 1876. The same year, Harry developed a friendship with the renowned landscape painter and interior designer Samuel Coleman, who was one of the earliest collectors of Chinese and Japanese art. Coleman shared his love of Asian art with Harry, especially Japanese textiles and Chinese porcelain, and Havemeyer fell in love with Asian art too. Coleman brought Havemeyer to the Centennial Exhibit in Philadelphia in 1876, where Harry was awed, and he made his first Asian purchases, buying carved ivory figures, Japanese lacquer boxes and silk brocades. Harry especially treasured Japanese textiles, and by age twenty-nine he became a discriminating collector of Japanese porcelains, rugs, textiles and gold or silver brocades. Coleman introduced Harry to the legendary New York designer Louis Comfort Tiffany and they became good friends. Quickly, Tiffany began advising Havemeyer on his art purchases.

In 1874, George Elder's widow collected her inheritance, and she brought the children, including nineteen-year-old Louisine, off to Paris. Louisine and her sister boarded and studied with the Del Sarte family, who rented rooms to Americans who wanted to learn French language and culture. Another guest in the Del Sarte home was Emily Sartain, an accomplished salon painter from Philadelphia. Sartaine became friendly with Louisine. Soon, Sartaine introduced the young New Yorker to the American artist Mary Cassatt who would have a profound influence on Louisine, who later wrote about Cassatt:

> When we first met in Paris she was very kind to me, showing me the splendid things in the great city, making them more splendid by opening my eyes to see their beauty through her own knowledge and appreciation. I felt that Miss Cassatt was the most intelligent woman I had ever met and I cherished every word she uttered and remembered almost every remark she made. It seemed to me, no one could see art more understandingly, feel it more deeply, or express themselves more clearly than she did. She opened her heart to me about art, while she showed me the great city.

By the age of twenty, Louisine had also acquired a taste for collecting art that was to remain with her all her days, and create a splendid legacy. Cassatt took Ms. Elder to a print shop where she saw Degas' work *Ballet Rehearsal*. The work was so avant-garde that Elder was not sure if she liked it or not, but she bought it on Cassatt's advice, becoming the first American ever to purchase one of his works. She had to borrow money from her two sisters to buy the painting. That same year, again at the urging of Cassatt, she became the first American to purchase a Monet when she bought *The Drawbridge, Amsterdam* for three hundred francs. She was destined to become one of the most influential American collectors of art with the fortune her future husband would earn through his domination of the sugar refining business.

Over the Bag Filter

Into the Bone Black Filter

One of the Centrifugal Machines

Filling the Dancing Barrels

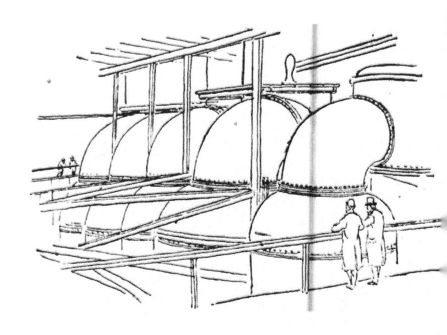

Five Immense Vacuum Pans

Opposite Page: Diagram Showing Location
of the American Sugar Refineries

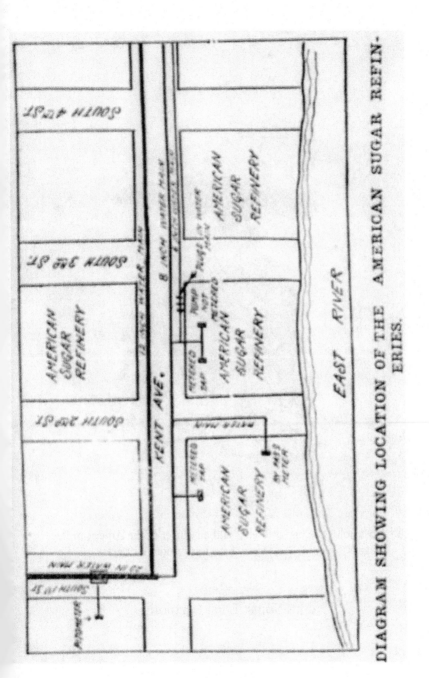

DIAGRAM SHOWING LOCATION OF THE AMERICAN SUGAR REFIN-
ERIES.

"The Trust holds the big umbrela," said an officer of the American Beet Sugar Company, "And we all have to sit under it or get wet."

Anti-Sugar Trust Cartoon

Henry Havemeyer

Claus Spreckles

Jack McAuliffe

Havemeyer Mansion, 66th Street

Interior of Havemeyer Mansion

Father Sylvester
Malone

Grahams Polley

Captain Martin Short

Hugh McLaughlin

Kent Avenue

Sugar Trust
Headquarters,
Wall Street

Saints Peter and Paul
Church

Havemeyer and Elder, 2017

Refinery View East River

Willis Hodges

Patrick H. McCarren,
1893

Oliver Spitzer

John Arbuckle

Lowell Palmer

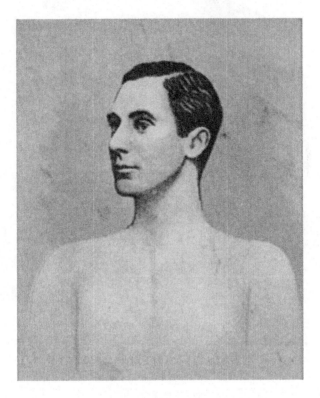

Sam Collyer

Sugar Workers Housing

Sugar Workers Tenement

Louisine Havemeyer

Theodore
Havemeyer

The Sugar King

Rembrandt Room

One of Brooklyn's Monster Sugar Refining Plants.

Unloading Raw Sugar

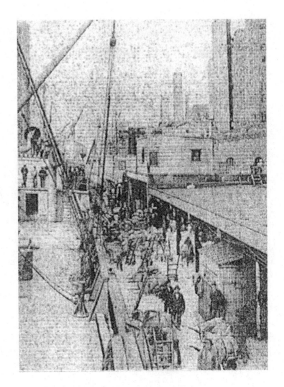

Unloading Raw Sugar

East River Waterfront

Williamsburg Bridge

The Refinery on Kent Avenue

Chapter Fifteen:
A Phoenix Rises from the Ashes of Despair - January 8, 1882

It had started like any other day in the refinery, but the Havemeyers knew that sugar refining was a dangerous and unpredictable business, and that disaster could suddenly strike. That cold morning a brisk wind blew in off the East River, while the shivering longshoremen prepared to unload the four steamers bobbing up and down in the water at their moorings in the East River alongside the Havemeyer and Elder Sugar refinery. The plant had six active wharves, each almost large enough to accommodate an ocean liner, to handle the tons of sugar that arrived every week from as far away as Brazil and Java. The ships did not show any evidence of the long winter voyage they had just completed sailing up from the Caribbean. The holds of each of the ships were laden with raw sugar. There were three Cuban steamers and one Jamaican. The Jamaican sugar had made the voyage contained in giant hogsheads, while the yellow Cuban sugar had traveled north in huge brown bags.

The raw sugar had been prepared back in the Caribbean long before its arrival in Brooklyn. The initial refining was done near the cane fields because freshly pressed cane juice fermented in less than twenty-four hours unless it was treated. Cane juice was pressed from the stalks by running them through a series of cast iron rollers; the juice was then cooked in large flat-bottomed copper pans, called clarifiers. Adding quicklime reduced the acidity of the cane juice, and as the impurities rose to the surface they were removed by skimming them off the surface of the liquid. The cleared liquid was siphoned into copper evaporating pans, where additional limewater was added to further reduce the acidity. The remaining liquid, called *treche*, was boiled again in smaller copper pans until it was reduced sufficiently to support the granulation of sugar. The thickened liquid was placed in cooling pans, which were stirred with wooden paddles. After it cooled, the sugar crystalized into small, irregular crystals or grains, which were suspended in the molasses. This sugar/molasses mixture was taken to the curing-house, where it was placed in hogsheads with small holes in the bottom; the holes were plugged with filters made of plantain stalks. The molasses slowly drained through the spongy stalks, leaving the sugar crystals in the bottom of the hogshead. After about three weeks, the sugar that remained in the barrels was packed into large hogsheads or shoveled into bags, each weighing between twelve hundred and two thousand pounds, which were shipped to the refineries as raw sugar.

Hundreds of burly longshoremen busied themselves with lifting the heavy sugar bags and hogsheads from the cargo holds to the wharf. Soon thousands of pounds of raw sugar lay in these containers on the wharf, waiting for hundreds of dockworkers to move them into the massive warehouse only a few steps away where literally millions of pounds of sugar was waiting for refining.

The massive, seven-building refinery was powered by a power plant burning two hundred tons of coal a day. Huge smokestacks, climbing high into the sky, burned the coal, converting it to the steam that powered the refining process. This single huge plant refined three quarters of the nation's refined sugar and accounted for one eighth of the world's sugar production. The refinery was so large that it contained needed a huge six-story-high warehouse to hold its immense output. The plant covered the waterfront from South Sixth Street to Grand Street, an area of one hundred fifty city lots with a total surface area of twelve acres. The heat from the massive amounts of burning coal made the engine room's thermometer, even on a winter's day like today, register one hundred twelve degrees. It is little wonder that this part of Williamsburg was called "Havemeyer town," even though other companies' refineries also lined the waterfront. The smell of burning coal and sugar filled the air, giving the whole neighborhood a distinctive aroma it would retain for years.

Almost three thousand men would labor today, turning that dark, moist, imported raw sugar into dry, white refined sugar. One hogshead of raw sugar required an elaborate eight-hour process to be refined. First, a chemist would test and weigh the sugar. Then, big, brawny workmen would tear open the hogsheads or bags of sugar, pouring brown sugar into huge vats on the ground floor of the plant where the sugar was boiled, mixing with syrup from a preceding batch. Later, after it had boiled, the sugary liquid was forced a hundred and fifty feet upwards by massive, powerful pumps to the top refinery floor to a different set of vats called blow ups. Sugar coated the metal on the catwalks surrounding these vats, making walking them slippery and treacherous for the workers who refined the sugar. The vats were fitted with mechanical stirrers with steam pipes coiled snake-like in their bottoms. They lay in rows down across the huge room, which measured two hundred and fifty feet in length and a hundred and fifty feet in width. The liquid boiled in the vats for twenty minutes until the mixing was done. Even on a cold winter's day the process generated huge amounts of heat, and the room was every bit as hot and humid as a Turkish sauna. The temperature reached ninety degrees, but the humidity was almost 100%, making everyone drip with sweat.

Next, the liquid drained through troughs into the floors below, collecting in long filtering bags underneath resembling long pipes, which were suspended from the floor above's roof. The bags contained an inner core of thick woven material and an outer core of sheathing. As the liquid passed through these massive filters, many of the physical impurities like sand and other debris were filtered out. The dark liquid slowly drained down to the floor below, where it was now ready to get whitened in huge pans, each weighing 80,000 pounds. These pans contained tons of animal boneblack, which was the remnants of animal bones that had been boiled, burned and ground. One floor of the refinery was covered with a hundred and four heads of the great filters whose bases lay two floors below. The filters were packed so tightly onto the floor that the firemen and stokers barely had room to shovel in the coal. The men wore little more than loincloths, so hot was the temperature from the boiling pans, and perspiration dripped constantly from every pore in the workers' bodies. As the liquid passed through the boneblack, it lost much of its coloration. Finally, water was forced into the pans, which pushed out the sugar. When the sugar emerged, it was a beautiful white liquid substance, and it was pumped into vats again where it was boiled to prepare it for the next step in the process.

The transparent liquid then entered five massive vacuum pans where it was further boiled. Each of the vacuum pans weighed eighty tons and required huge amounts of coal to fire it. Again, this step in the refining process produced sauna-like humidity and scorching temperatures. Massive condensers worked above the pans, turning the air sucked out of the pans into liquid. The vacuum created by the devices allowed the liquid to boil at a much lower temperature, and the sugar crystalized far faster than it would have without being in a vacuum. In these huge cauldrons the solution was whipped, beaten, flayed and hurled into grain. This flagellation process lasted three quarters of an hour, and was so violent that it resembled a caged cyclone. Each of the vacuum pans was sixteen feet in diameter, and thirty-two feet high, holding eighty-five tons of solution. The condensers required huge amounts of water to cool the air coming out of the pans, and 20,000,000 gallons of East River water was extracted from the river, run up a sluiceway over the condensers and then the water returned to the river.

The pans then discharged the crystalized sugar into six massive machines on the floor below. The men who worked at these centrifuges had to endure the worst suffering in the plant because the machines gave off so much heat that temperatures reached one hundred thirty degrees. The nearly naked workers all constantly wiped themselves off with huge towels in their battle against the massive perspiration that poured out of their bodies. Tiny perforations in the sides of the centrifuge allowed the liquid to spin off while the sugar remained inside. The sugar then dropped through the bottom of the centrifuge into a number of bins that extended down two stories. No sooner did it drop into these cooling bins than the sugar was then lifted up four stories to pass through sets of rollers, taking any remaining lumps out of the sugar. If the sugar needed to be granulated, it then passed through hollow cylinders thirty-five feet long and eight feet wide. Fans at one end of the cylinder drew in hot air, and as the cylinder slowly revolved, the sugar fell through it, becoming granulated as it passed from the beginning to the end of the long tube.

Each day Havemeyer and Elder refined four-and-a-half-million pounds of sugar in this way, which filled some 13,000 barrels, but even one more step was required to ensure that the sugar was packed as tightly as possible in the barrel. The sugar had to be jiggled on a moving stand, as the constant motion packed the sugar tightly into the barrel.

Now that the sugar had been refined, it was sent on a conveyor belt high up the plant to a bridge that crossed Kent Street and into the mammoth warehouse where it was temporarily stored. The sugar was then sent to the Palmer's Dock where it was put in freight cars that traveled on trains around the country.

The Havemeyers were well aware of the ever-present danger of fire in the refinery, and the refinery had been fireproofed as much as possible to minimize the risk of fire. Sugar clouds, though, often ignited, causing huge fires. The presence of steam, thousands of moving parts that could cause sparks in the refinery and the highly flammable sugar all made fire a grave risk. For a quarter century they had refined huge amounts of sugar without a fire, but their luck would run out that January day.

None of the sugar unloaded that morning in the plant would ever make it to market. At about three o' clock in the afternoon, Theodore Havemeyer made his customary inspection of the plant and noticed nothing suspicious. Three watchmen, two superintendents and two assistants remained in the refinery. The night shift was just appearing at four o' clock when watchman Edward Haman began to smell smoke, and found the flames in a storeroom on the refinery's first floor. Dense smoke quickly filled the room, and flames soon leapt from storeroom. The watchman pulled an alarm that alerted the workers in the plant, and also sent a signal to the fire department. About fifty hands on duty at the plant rushed to refinery, grabbing hoses and attempting to put out the blaze. There were precious minutes of indecision which wasted critical time in finding and turning on the water spigot for the hose. Four engines responded to the first alarm, and four additional companies also answered the second alarm, but twelve minutes had elapsed since the fire was reported. This interval, though, had given the fire time to spread. The fireboat *Havemeyer* from Manhattan even appeared on the scene, trying to douse the flames, but all the firefighters' efforts were in vain.

The fire moved both upwards and downwards at an alarming speed. Dense masses of potentially flammable vapor poured into the areas where the workers were now using the hose to douse the blaze. Other workers were removing stacks of records, while some others were trying to wheel out barrels of sugar; however, soon choking fumes reached the area where they were unloading the barrels, and they were left with no choice but to abandon the plant.

Outside the plant the first fire companies quickly deployed, frantically setting up ladders, while spreading out hoses. As the firemen and company employees looked up, they realized that it was probably already too late. Fueled by tons of sugar the fire was racing upwards, and flames could already be seen in many of the upper windows. The heat from the fire was so intense that many of the firefighters developed blisters on their faces. Firefighters had to move back from the building's façade due to the amazing heat of the fire. A number of vats of alcohol blew up, sounding like cannon fire. As the sugar burned, it glowed in a rainbow of colors, the beauty of the flames masking their deadly effectiveness.

Chief Smith, immediately realizing the scope of the blaze, called in a third and fourth alarm as other companies rushed to the scene. The flames had reached the pan filter rooms, adding coal to the already hot blaze. The flames raced upwards in the seven stories that faced Kent Avenue. As the flames reached higher and higher, they could now be seen in other neighborhoods. Soon, the alarm bells and the shooting flames attracted crowds of fascinated onlookers. A brilliant glow of flame filled the foggy night sky, which could be clearly seen far away in Queens and even in northern Manhattan.

The firefighters were hampered by a lack of hydrants close to the great refinery. They soon realized that wind had the potential to spread the conflagration to other sugarhouses, and there was the real possibility that all Williamsburg could burn down. There was a covered second story bridge connecting the refinery to the boiler house on South Second Street that posed a huge danger of allowing the fire to spread. Chief Nevins, who had just arrived on the scene, ordered the bridge taken down, and the firefighters had just commenced cutting the span from the burning building when the burning refinery walls began to sway, signaling the danger that they would collapse. A panic ensued, and the firemen instantaneously abandoned their task, fleeing from the bucking walls. Only a few seconds later, three stories of brick and mortar came crashing down the to street, severing the bridge, while fortuitously helping the firefighters limit the spread of the flames. Martin Short and the other officers from the precinct arrived to keep the large crowds who came to gawk at the blaze away from danger.

A few minutes later, the steam pipes burst, and the hiss of their exploding was loud enough to be heard above the din of the flames. Realizing that the job at hand was to save the new refinery building on the other side of the street, Chiefs Smith and Nevins deployed their men inside and outside the structure across the street. He sent a team up the winding inner staircase with a long hose, and another up the fire escape on the exterior of the building. Both crews did excellent work fighting the fires that threatened to jump the street.

Suddenly, a massive section from the top of the old refinery came crashing to ground in the shape of a giant V. Much of the falling material hit the new refinery, engulfing it in flame, and threatening to create a second inferno.

Then, the roof of the old refinery collapsed, and a gush of flame shot up like lava from a spewing volcano. The flames from the burning refinery soared over the top of the ruins, lighting up the river, and there was a lurid beauty to the ghastly spectacle that attracted huge crowds along the Manhattan shoreline watching spellbound by the blaze.

About six o'clock, the remnants of the wall of the

old refinery facing Kent Street, which had previously crumbled at the top, buckled and collapsed in a deafening roar as a great cloud of smoke rose from the street. When the cloud disappeared, onlookers could see the entire interior of the doomed refinery. The fire burned green, fueled by the chemicals that only a short while ago helped refine the sugar. The south wall finally gave way, crumbling to the ground and showering the street below with brick. It soon became apparent that the danger of the fire spreading had passed, and that the fire would slowly burn itself out, consuming the remaining parts of the massive refinery in the process.

Then, just as it seemed that the fire was contained, flames broke out in the new refinery, fueled by the collapse of burning wooden tanks on the building's roof, but the firemen stationed there fought heroically and contained the blaze. A half-hour later, they had doused most of the fires in the new refinery, and finally the danger had truly passed.

Theodore Havemeyer, who had built the refinery twenty-five years earlier, helplessly witnessed the lurid scene in total horror. Interviewed by a throng of reporters, Havemeyer was asked to identify the cause and to estimate the extent of the damage. Havemeyer could put forward no theory explaining how the fire had started. He put the figure of the total loss at $1,500,000. He also reckoned that the value of the plant was $250,000 and the machinery inside was worth $750,000. He further estimated that the sugar stores inside the plant were worth $500,000. He further informed the reporters that a thousand two hundred men who worked in the old refinery would be put out of work. The refinery had been insured with several policies, but its value was so great that its total value could never have been fully insured.

The Havemeyer family quickly gathered to plan how to react to the catastrophe. To make matters worse, on news of the fire the price of sugar surged up, a boon to their competitors whose profits would soar. Immediately after the fire, Fredrick, aged seventy-five, his two sons Theodore, Harry and Charles Senff sat down to craft a response. The cost of rebuilding would be huge, running to $7,000,000 and stretching the resources of the wealthy clan to the limit. There was, however, no hesitation, and they all agreed not only to rebuild, but also to create the largest, most efficient refinery in the world. Fredrick put his entire fortune into the rebuilding project, even selling off his beloved Throggs Neck estate Beau Rivage.

Just down the river from the ashes of the refinery builders had been at work for a dozen years constructing the Brooklyn Bridge. The new refinery would rise higher than the towers of the bridge, but also be built in a much shorter time frame. It had to be done quickly, and there was no margin of error. Every day that the refinery was offline was a day that their competitors gained a competitive advantage, and Havemeyer and Elder lost a huge amount of money.

Rebuilding was not only a financial strain, but also a mental and physical one. Theodore, who suffered from ill health, overworked himself, as did Senff and plant manager Ernest Gerbracht. Finally, a year and a half later, the new refinery was built, but there was uncertainty about how many glitches might remain in the complicated process of refining sugar on such a huge scale. Everyone waited anxiously for the first test run of the plant to see the results, which turned out to be a failure. Management panicked when the centrifuges installed in the new plant vibrated too violently, shattering the brick arches that supported them each time they were fired up. The builder of the plant threw up his hands, and it seemed that if the centrifuges did not work, then the entire plant would be useless. Long delays loomed; however, they discovered that when the centrifuges were readjusted to allow for more vibration their vibrations did not shatter the arches, and then they functioned perfectly. The first raw sugar was successfully refined, and the year and a half of anxiety was finally over.

Eighteen months after the fire, the new plant was finished, and nothing else like it existed anywhere in the world. It was a state-of-the-art building. The new refinery rose majestically ten stories above the East River, compared by some to a castle towering above the Rhine River. It was built entirely of pressed brick that was designed to be fireproof. The walls were two feet thick at the top, and four feet thick at their base. The filter house of the new refinery rose thirteen stories above the street, and was full of the most cutting-edge technology of the day. The building contained a hundred and eight cast iron filters and twenty-four centrifuges, each sixteen feet in diameter.

Most impressively, the new refinery was designed to refine 3,000,000 pounds of sugar a day, faster and cheaper than any other refinery in the world. After the construction of the new plant, the firm became the only American company that could produce soft sugar. It could also manufacture sugar cubes as well as dark brown sugar, entirely new sugar products. The new refinery could refine twice as much sugar as the largest refinery of their nearest competitors. The firm had not only survived the fire, but it had even emerged from the fire far more dominant.

The calamity placed even more strain on the already irritable and explosive Harry. He drank even more heavily and grew abusive. His marriage, which was already in trouble, collapsed under the strain of the rebuilding effort, and he filed for divorce in September of 1882. Louise would never recover from the trauma of the divorce, and she would die three years after it, from what reportedly was a broken heart. It seemed that his chances for a happy family had been decimated, but for Harry love, like the burned refinery itself, would quickly rise from the ashes of his divorce.

Chapter Sixteen:
Strikes - 1886

The Havemeyers had emerged triumphant from the ordeal of the fire and the plant reconstruction, but they had also paid a heavy personal price. The eighteen months of round-the-clock, high-anxiety work required to rebuild the charred ruins of the refinery had taken a toll on everyone in the firm, but perhaps none more than Theodore Havemeyer who worked like a fiend during the reconstruction. The stress of directing the rebuilding of the huge new plant and overseeing the installation of the monstrous machinery in the refinery proved too taxing on his already poor health, and he planned to take a long European holiday in 1885 to recuperate.

The stress of rebuilding also put a severe strain on his relationship with his volatile and demanding brother Harry, who deeply resented the news of his brother's trip to Europe. The two brothers argued vociferously. Harry felt that his brother's place was in the refinery, and the fight between the two siblings became so acrimonious that it threatened to destroy the partnership. Harry grew even more furious with his brother when he learned that Theodore had become a partner in a competing refinery in Philadelphia. Considering it a betrayal of loyalty to the family business, Harry accused his brother of divulging valuable trade secrets to the Pennsylvania competitors, which Theodore vehemently denied. The dispute was only settled by the intervention of by the seventy-eight-year-old patriarch Fredrick Havemeyer, who prevented the break up of the family business, and forged an unsteady truce between the brothers.

With the re-emergence of the larger and more cost-efficient Williamsburg plant, sugar output increased, price decreased and competition became desperate. The margin between the cost of raw and refined sugar dropped to a new low, and fluctuated wildly in relation to the market price of raw sugar. Lower prices were driving competing firms to the wall, and these firms began dumping sugar on the market, and even selling at a loss. The year 1886 witnessed the bankruptcy of eighteen sugar plants. The strain of selling sugar in the fiercely competitive market made Harry even more irritable, and he showered his wrath on those around him. It took all Harry's guile and savvy to sell the sugar the firm produced profitably. Still, Havemeyer and Elder, because of the efficiency of the new plant, emerged as the one firm who could still make a profit, despite the new lower cost of refined sugar in the saturated market. Remarkably, although there was cutthroat competition in the sugar market, the firm still managed to make a 5 to 6% return on its investments in 1886.

Rightfully, some of the firm's profits should have gone to the workers in the form of increased pay and benefits, but the Havemeyers proved to be stingy, paying plant workers just fourteen and a half cents per hour. Workers in their plants were addressed not by name, but by number, reflecting the prevailing firm's indifferent attitude towards its workers. Because the area was a magnet for immigration, the plant could employ newly arrived immigrants who did not speak English at sweat shop wages. The Havemeyers showed little concern for the thousands of men who were helping them become millionaires, and regularly hired newer immigrants as replacements for established workers when the refinery's workers demanded higher wages, shorter hours and safer conditions.

It had been the workers, and not management, who suffered most of all during the eighteenth months rebuilding took. One thousand five hundred were laid off, and they had to fend for themselves without the benefit of any safety net to help them and their families. The high efficiency of the new plant hurt the thousands of workers who toiled in its hellish heat. The winter slack season when many got laid off now lasted longer, and worst of all, the efficiency in production, as well as a surplus of sugar on the market, meant that the plant laid off more frequently, usually without any advance notice. When the plant suddenly and unexpectedly shut, the shocked workers received no severance pay or any kind of wages, causing extreme hardship, especially on their impoverished families who lived in the overcrowded tenements that had sprung up all over Williamsburg. During these frequent closures, families struggled to get by on their meager savings.

When the plant was opened just before the Civil War, much of the staff consisted of Germans who lived in tenements in the German Dutch Town ward. German and English were the two languages spoken in the plant, but by the mid 1880s, Poles and other Slavs had increasingly replaced Germans, especially in the hardest, most dangerous and least-paying jobs.

The Polish immigrant refinery workers were denigrated in a *Brooklyn Daily Eagle* expose on their lives, which vilified them as people who would rather have a few gallons of whiskey than an office. The newspaper also maliciously commented on the fears of the Irish and Germans of the Polish immigrant worker, noting, "They know that he is willing to work for whatever he can get and that he will do faithful service without an attempt to change his lot through the service of a labor union—that is until he is absolutely in control, and then you cannot say exactly what he will do for out west he has shown himself to be capable of nasty conduct."

The refinery workers lived in slum blocks made up of dilapidated, wood-shingle, three and four-story tenement houses, looking like oversized frame houses, which had sprung up in the nineteenth century close to the neighborhood's refineries, factories, warehouses, breweries, food processing plants and foundries. The tenements had no indoor plumbing or central heat, and residents were forced to use putrid outhouses in the back yard. *The Brooklyn Daily Eagle* reported on the overcrowded, unsanitary tenements where the Poles lived, painting a grim picture of their squalid living arrangements. The paper noted that there was a "lower sort of tenement" occupied less frequently by Germans, and more often by Poles. The reporter described "the wretched barracks" of the

Poles, which lacked adequate air and light. The article also described the abominable odor from the chamber pots in the hall, and painted a picture of these tenements as health and fire hazards that posed risks for Williamsburg.

The Brooklyn Daily Eagle also described the seedy rooming house where many single Polish refinery workers lived, noting that many lived in mansions of faded gentility near the plant that were deplorable for their decay. The paper described the once-elegant colonnaded houses that were now "faded, rusty and shabby." It further described the bareness of the rooms and the lack of a furnace, as well as the fact that rooming houses charged extra for heat in the winter. The report noted that the rooms contained curtains of the cheapest cotton, faded carpets, matting in the bedroom and oil lamps for light because gaslight was too expensive for the underpaid sugar workers. Finally, the *Daily Eagle* noted the lack of running water in any of the rooms, and the musty smell and putrid odor of the halls.

The plant was refining sugar in a time before the government set regulations to ensure worker safety. Work in the plant was highly dangerous for the three thousand or so workers who toiled there. Workers could be killed or injured in a variety of ways and there was no system of workers' compensation. Untested machinery often led to explosions that caused horrific injuries, or even fatalities. Workers could be scalded by steam, or a falling elevator could crush them. Workers could impale themselves by falling on a hook, or they could get pinned under a falling sugar bag. They could also fall off slippery catwalks, or get caught by machines like George Havemeyer. Sugar dust also hurt the workers' health. Breathing the dust over seventy hours a week caused lung ailments, and many of the workers developed chronic coughs, and had trouble breathing. The dust also produced skin rashes that sometimes covered the workers' almost totally exposed bodies.

Even if a sugar worker did not fall victim to the many kinds of accidents that could disable him, then the constant exposure to the intense heat of the plant might destroy him. The sauna-like temperatures quickly wrecked strong men who went into the plant. Outsiders could recognize sugar workers because of their gauntness and pallid skin tone. Sugar workers quickly appeared physically drained and prematurely aged. To help the workers to replenish the huge amounts of salt the sugar workers sweated out on their 10-or-12-hour shifts, the firm served beer at cost, charging the workers a penny for a pound of beer. Management arranged to have beer brought into the refinery several times a day from a local brewery.

It is little wonder that the saloons surrounding the plant did a huge business, or that heat-exhausted workers drank excessively. Often the men spent large amounts of their meager wages overindulging in beer, bringing hardship on their dependent families who relied on them for the basic necessities of life.

Father Malone could have defended the sugar workers in his congregation, but he did not. He was especially critical of men who drank to excess, and blamed the drinking workers for the poverty many families experienced. Perhaps his close friendship with Theodore Havemeyer and his wife, to whom he was confessor, colored his view of the Havemeyers' treatment of their employees. The pastor also might have been influenced by the huge gift of $35,000 Theodore Havemeyer gave Father Malone four years previously when he visited Ireland. When asked about the possibility of a strike Father Malone said that the workers should be grateful for their employment in the refinery, and he uttered not even one word in criticism of Havemeyer and Elder.

To maximize profit, the plant never fully shut down refining, running three hundred and sixty-five days a year, twenty-four hours a day. The plant even stayed open on the hottest days of the year, despite the gruesome reality that the extreme heat and humidity, without adequate ventilation, would lead to deaths. On scorching days, hundreds of sugar workers were driven to the verge of insanity. On searing twelve-hour-long days some firemen, driven to insanity by shoveling coal in the extreme heat and humidity, threw themselves into the East River from the top of the factory. During these hellish days, hundreds of workers succumbed to the heat, often passing out at their stations. On one particularly hot day, there were eight heat related deaths. On another scorching day, more than 600 fell prostrate from the heat. On another occasion, a third of the entire refinery workforce, some 400 workers, fainted with the heat. Because passing out on hot days was so common, the refinery set up an ambulance system to bring prostrate workers to the local hospital, but sometimes treatment came too late.

Newspapers became aware of the suffering of the sugar workers, and tried to gain entrance to the plant, but they were denied entry. Ernest Gerbracht, the plant manager, stated in *The Brooklyn Daily Eagle* "Whenever we see a reporter here our impulse is to throw him out. What do you want to write anything about the men for their wages are paid as regularly as any place in the country and when they get hurt we have a place to take care of them. Isn't' that enough?" In an effort to prevent the press from exposing the terrible conditions inside the plant, Gerbracht, practiced a deliberate policy of employing men who could not communicate in English, and as a result, over the years the plant had become less German and more Slavic with many immigrant Poles, Bohemians and Slovaks composing the majority of the refinery workers.

In 1886, the workers of Havemeyer and Elder and the other Williamsburg sugar plants struck for better pay and union recognition. Three thousand men went on strike, including refinery workers, longshoremen and coopers. The strike hit all the sugar refineries from the Havemeyer and Elder refinery in Williamsburg to the Havemeyer refinery, run by a cousin, at the northern tip of Greenpoint. The goal of the strike was a reduction from a 12 to 10 hour day and a raise of the daily wage to $1.75, but all of the sugar refinery owners refused to meet the demands of the strikers, and they were adamantly opposed to any union recognition.

The refinery owners were confident of their ability to resist the strike because of the refined sugar reserves they had accumulated, and their awareness that their lowly paid workers lacked the financial resources to remain on strike long, especially because so many of the sugar workers had large, hungry families. On April 26, just after the strike began, there was a secret meeting of the factory owners and managers in the offices of Havemeyer and Elder. They were united in their determination not to let the union interfere in their running of their firms. They were also determined to hold out against the strike until they could win, and prove themselves to be the absolute and unquestioned masters of their companies. William Dick, president of the Williamsburg sugar refinery firm Dick and Meyer, showed his contempt for his workers, his thoughts on hiring replacement workers, stating and the need of the police, stating, "We can get all the men we want to work for us, if we were only guaranteed protection."

The newspapers all focused on the violence of the strikers, and of the widespread influence of communist agitators, while they generally neglected the grievances of the workers. In one of the few admissions that the workers had any legitimate grievances, *The Brooklyn Daily Eagle* quoted a Republican strike witness who reflected the xenophobia inherent in the newspapers' coverage saying:

I am sure that the sugar men have been underpaid. I

sympathize with them, but I hold that American citizens are the only ones who dictate as to American prices. If men make trouble on First Street or anywhere else let the police ask them for their citizens' papers. If they fail to show them I hold that the authorities can send them back to their own country, just as they have the right to send back pauper immigrants from Castle Garden. This is not a country that can be ruled by aliens.

The New York Times also accented the violent foreign element amongst the strikers, stating:

The blood red ribbon of the communist, pinned to the lapel of the striking German, Austrian and Polander gives the clue to the reason why riotous proceedings were instituted so quickly, and in each case on so slight a provocation. The communists with which this section of Brooklyn is infested gloried in their defiance of the legally constituted authorities and openly boasted to this Times reporter that they would either have their demands complied with or else would, if necessary, destroy the property of their former employees with the torch. So violent were the strikers, so defiant of all authority, save that of their leaders and so fearful were the police authorities that they would carry out their threats to kill and burn, that all police reserves were on duty last night, guarding the property between first street and the river, from Second Street up to Rush Street.

The Brooklyn Daily Eagle also took the side of management and police against the strikers, highlighting the communist agitators amongst the strikers. The paper noted that red-scarfed communists probably composed 10% of the strikers and claimed they were "spoiling for a fight and seem especially eager to attack the police and destroy the property of the refiners." The *Eagle* claimed that every one of them carried a knife, and that they were a dangerous set. The newspaper also claimed that the police were "compelled to use the most heroic methods" against them, and that is why there were so many bloody police clubs.

The police, including Detective Martin Short, manned the dangerous picket lines that separated the hundreds of angry picketing workers from the refineries. Short must have felt like a soldier again, recalling the battles he fought two decades previously, because the conflicts between the police and the strikers on the streets resembled pitched battles to the heavily outnumbered police who often confronted hundreds of angry protestors, armed with stones, bricks and sometimes even guns. In the April 23rd edition of *The New York Times*, the paper described three riots that the police had to contend with. The paper described the heroism of the police, who were outnumbered twenty to one by the three thousand strikers. The first riot happened at North Sixth Street when a wagon full of raw sugar tried to enter the Dick and Meyer plant. When the police tried to escort the wagon through the picket lines, the strikers showered them with bricks, cobblestones and clubs. The *Times* reported that each officer was knocked to the ground, and it appeared for a moment that the strikers would win, but the police managed to regain their feet, while using their clubs to beat back the angry rioters.

South of Grand Street at four o'clock, there was a similar incident when a teamster tried to drive a wagon full of empty barrels through a "surging, surly, growling mob" comprising striking sugar workers and longshoremen. The leader of the strike, John Engel, made an appeal for calm, but again, the *Times* noted that communists wearing red ribbons fomented violence despite Engel's pleas. An officer's demand that a striker move across the street led the officer to scuffle with one of the strikers. Suddenly, the officer was knocked to the ground and surrounded by a "howling" mob of hundreds." The police who had to charge the mob again were pelted with cobblestones and other missiles. The *Times* described how one of the strikers was only prevented from braining an officer knocked to the ground by another officer who cracked the attacker's skull with a club. Six rioters were arrested during the unrest and charged with rioting.

The worst violence of the day happened at the Havemeyer refinery in nearby Greenpoint when a striking worker attempted to enter the refinery. Prevented from entering by Officer Delaney, a scuffle again ensued and dozens of the strikers came to the aid of their fellow striker. Officer Strickey came the aid of Delaney, and beat the strikers with his club, but he was also knocked the ground. It even seemed for a moment that the two officers would be killed. Delaney, however, reached for his revolver, leveling it at the heads of the mob. Someone across the road shouted out "shoot," and Delaney discharged his weapon, hitting one of the strikers in the arm. Officer Strickey also pulled out his weapon, firing into the air.

A group of police officers rushed the mob with clubs drawn and "the fight became desperate." The *Times* article said that "The strikers were, with scarcely an exception, men of savage instinct and they fought like tigers." The strikers, according to the *Times*, used cart rungs, bale sticks, and whatever they could get their hands on, in a desperate struggle that left two officers unconscious.

Detective Martin Short was assigned one of the most dangerous tasks in the conflict: arresting one of the leaders of the strike. Short arrested the president of the Sugar Workers Committee, John Engel, on a charge of incitement to violence. The arrest stemmed from a claim that Engel paid a striker to beat up a scab.

Over time, the inherent advantages of management prevailed, and Havemeyer and the other owners of the sugar factories emerged victorious. Management simply waited out the striking workers, their factories and property protected by the police. The destitute strikers, who had families to feed, quickly ran out of money, and they were soon forced to return to work without any of their major demands being met. The leaders of the strike were blackballed, and the defeated workers continued to toil in the inferno-like conditions of the refinery without the protection of a union.

Some of the workers in frustration turned to arson to get revenge. In June of 1887, an arsonist set a fire that burned the thirteen-story sugar refinery in Greenpoint to the ground. In May of 1887, Detective Short arrested a man for setting fire to Palmer's train depot at North Fifth Street. A few days later, Palmer's cooperage also went up in flames with a $600,000 loss under suspicious circumstances.

The owners of the sugar factories had united against a common enemy, and they had defeated the workers. The following year they would again unite to create an entity that would make them rich beyond their wildest dreams. The leader of that cartel, Henry Havemeyer, would not only become extremely wealthy, but would also be hailed nationally as "The Sugar King."

Chapter Seventeen:
Bonds of Trust?

By 1887, there was chaos in the sugar market. The profit margin on refining sugar hit its lowest mark ever, down to under a penny profit per pound. The fierce competition in the sugar market, and the wild fluctuations in price, severely limited the profits that even successful sugar refiners like Harry Havemeyer could earn. All the refiners across America faced the same contradiction of a saturated market: the only way to make more money as the profit margin shrank was to refine more sugar, which drove the price of sugar down even further, creating a vicious downward spiral.

Harry Havemeyer wanted to have high, stable prices for refined sugar, which meant that he and the other major refiners had to come to some kind of agreement on the amount of sugar produced and its cost. Already by the early 1880s, Harry Havemeyer was looking for a model for a sugar-producing cartel that would drastically limit sugar production and raise prices. Many of the sugar refiners were Williamsburg- based, German Americans who not only shared a common culture, but also shared a mutual interest in raising the price of refined sugar to reap profits. In 1881, they forged a verbal agreement to set a standard wholesale price for refined sugar and to limit production. The firms in the agreement were Havemeyer and Elder, Mathieson of Jersey City and the Weichers family, but it quickly fell apart because the agreement was impossible to enforce, and the temptation to cheat was too great.

If Havemeyer needed an example of a refining business that had formed a cartel to control both production and price, then there was one right in the neighborhood. It was America's largest company, Standard Oil, which refined the majority of its oil on and around the East River and Newtown Creek.

Harry Havemeyer studied Standard Oil, seeing in it a model to form a sugar-producing cartel that would create a national sugar refining monopoly. America's richest man, John D. Rockefeller, who by the 1870s was already a presence in North Brooklyn, set up Standard Oil. Rockefeller had his eyes set on buying up the Astral Oil Refinery located on the East River at North Fourteenth Street. In 1867, Charles Pratt had opened, the

Astral Oil Works there, but seven years later Rockefeller, who wanted to gain complete control over the oil refining business, issued him an ultimatum. Rockefeller offered Pratt and his partner Henry H. Rodgers the stark choice of selling out to Rockefeller's Standard Oil, or facing annihilation, because Rockefeller had the capability to sell at a loss indefinitely in order to drive Pratt's firm into bankruptcy.

Rogers was an amazing businessman, and he and Havemeyer must have met and discussed the Standard Oil Trust, where he was a vice president. Earlier in life, Rogers and a partner contracted a huge debt to Pratt. The partner skipped out on the debt, but in 1866, Rogers told Pratt he would take personal responsibility for the entire debt. Pratt was so impressed that he immediately hired Rogers for his refinery. It would prove to be a brilliant hiring decision. Pratt made Rogers foreman of the refinery, with a promise of a partnership if sales ran over $50,000 a year, which they did. Rogers worked fiendishly, often sleeping outside beside the huge tanks on the East River, and moved steadily up from foreman to manager, and finally to refinery superintendent. He so far exceeded Pratt's substantial sales goal that Pratt invited Rogers to become a full partner in the new firm of Charles Pratt and Company. Rapidly, Rogers became, in the words of Elbert Hubbard, Pratt's "hands and feet and eyes and ears." While working with Pratt, Rogers invented an improved way of separating naphtha, a light oil similar to kerosene, from crude oil, and was granted U.S. Patent #120,539 on October 31, 1871. The patent helped make the firm huge amounts of money.

Pratt built his refinery on what was once the most beautiful place in Williamsburg, the willow tree groves at the mouth of Bushwick Creek. Pratt's refinery would do more than merely destroy a grove of trees. Pratt and other refiners killed all the aquatic life in the East River and Newtown Creek, changing local waterways from limpid bodies of fresh water into malodorous polluted eyesores that blotted the landscape, but made men fortunes.

Eventually, Rockefeller forced Pratt and Rogers to merge with Standard Oil, and Rockefeller now acquired a huge local presence with many refineries on the East River and Newtown Creek. The negotiations were tense because Rockefeller had the upper hand, but Rogers coolly formulated terms, which guaranteed financial security and jobs for Pratt and himself. Rockefeller thought Pratt weak and a pushover, but he greatly admired Rogers' tenacity and negotiating skills, seeing in him the kind of ruthless manager that Standard Oil needed. In 1874, Rockefeller quietly accepted the offer on the exact terms Rogers had laid out.

In 1881, Standard Oil was reorganized as the Standard Oil Trust. By 1885, the three main men of Standard Oil Trust were John D. Rockefeller, his brother William, and Rogers, who had emerged as its top financial strategist. By 1890, Rogers was a vice president of Standard Oil, and chairman of the organization's operating committee. Rogers soon became the driving force in Standard Oil, America's richest corporation. Standard's model of organization and business tactics would serve as a model for Havemeyer, who would forge a "Sugar Trust" patterned on Standard Oil.

Rockefeller's lawyers created a new legal device called a trust, which consisted of a group of trustees, the functional equivalent of a board of directors, in whom stock of different corporations could be vested, giving trustees absolute control over management of properties. Standard Oil certificates became the first significant securities traded on Wall Street. Rockefeller's trust could control the market, and the price of oil, by closing either temporarily or permanently inefficient plants, a feature, which would lie at the heart of the Sugar Trust, Havemeyer would create.

All the major sugar refiners who would join the

Trust shared four broad goals. Firstly, they wanted to run their companies with fewer administrative costs, and reduce the costs of refining sugar. Secondly, they wanted to introduce the latest cutting-edge technology, and use the most efficient methods possible in refining sugar. Thirdly, they wanted to make sure their workers did not form unions that would drive up their labor costs. Finally, they all wanted to sell sugar at the highest price possible, so the basis for an agreement based on mutual interest existed.

While Havemeyer was busy with the daily business of selling sugar, one of the officers in Havemeyer and Elder, a member of the board of directors, John Searles, devoted himself exclusively to hammering out an agreement to create a sugar-refining cartel. Searles, the son of a Protestant minister from Westchester, had gained a central position in Havemeyer and Elder because of his knowledge of the sugar business and of the intricacies of corporate law. Searles spent long hours convincing Havemeyer that a trust was the only viable solution to the problem of overproduction in the sugar industry. Although Harry agreed with Searles on the issue of overproduction, he was reluctant to cede control of his plant to a group, which he feared could be dominated by his competitors. He sat down with his brother and Charles Senff to discuss the possibility of joining the Trust.

Havemeyer finally told Searles to bring the major producers together to work out the details of forming the Trust. A brilliant Philadelphia-born corporate lawyer named John Dos Pasos worked out the legal formulation of the Trust. One of the biggest goals of the Trust was to keep outsiders from discovering the Trust's secrets, more specifically that they were colluding to raise the price of sugar for the American consumer. Dos Pasos pointed out to the sugar refiners that if they formed a corporation, when they tried to take over another refinery their acquisition would be a matter of public record that was open to scrutiny, but with a trust they could avoid examination of their business moves.

Dos Pasos explained how the Trust functioned saying:

> Assume that certain persons desire to become owners of some manufacturing business or commercial enterprise, which is owned by say six corporations, having bought shares of these companies. The six get together and make what is called a trust agreement, which recites the terms under which the securities are held, that is the stock. The shares of these six constituent are taken and placed in the

hands of a trustee who has no actual or real ownership, except that he is a custodian. The shares accordingly belong to the trustee to administer the trust. The trustee in turn issued to the former holders of the stock a receipt called a trust certificate.

Because no single individual or group of owners owned all the sugar refining properties that were to be consolidated, the terms of the Trust agreement were vital. Helping Dos Pasos draft the agreement was the personal legal counsel for the Havemeyers, John Parsons. He explained to Harry how the Trust would begin. Each firm entering the Trust turned over its capital stock to a board designated as the Sugar Refineries Company. Since four of the refineries entering the Trust were partnerships these four firms took the added step of reorganizing themselves as corporations. Each firm would conduct business just as it had done before, but henceforth the company was subject to the overriding authority of the trustee board. The board would consist of eleven members who would each serve seven years. Harry made sure that he and his brother would serve on the board, and select the other board members. A simple majority of the board decided all questions and it could also fill vacancies on the board. Aside from dividends, the only right reserved for the actual owners was the right to vote during the annual meetings each June to replace or continue the terms of expiring board members.

The biggest stumbling block and bone of contention was determining the value of each of the companies entering the Trust and what percentage of Trust profits they were entitled to receive. They set up a committee to appraise the value of the various properties being consolidated into the Trust, and then they distributed to the stockholders of each company Trust stock certificates in the same ratio as the value of their refinery to the value of the whole Trust. Negotiations on the value of the plants were kept secret from other plant owners because the leaked information would drive up the prices of the properties the Trust was buying. Companies, though, were happy to turn over their stock to the Trust because they received Trust stock certificates worth four times the nominal value of the shares they surrendered.

Realizing that they were creating a business organization of dubious legality, the partners put as little in writing as possible. Julius Strusberg of the Brooklyn Sugar Refinery not only eagerly agreed to join, but also to convince the other refiners to enter the Trust. It is little wonder why he was eager since his firm had lost $200,000 in the first half of 1887 alone. Joseph

Mollner of the North River Refinery, which entered the trust, explained why they needed little discussion or persuasion, "We were all practical men of sugar-refining and as far as we were concerned we did not consider any discussion necessary. We all knew that the only way to make sugar-refining pay was to stop over-production." Another refiner, Claus Doscher, explained why he was eager to join the Trust: "We were handling not our own money, but other people's money, and we could not go on losing other people's money."

One of the chief goals of the Trust was to avoid publicity and public scrutiny. The initial plan was to limit the number of stockholders to just twenty-seven people, all of whom understood the value of silence. They agreed that the Trust would function differently than a corporation, which shared information with its shareholders. The Trust would not inform its shareholders of the decisions it took. The shareholders understood that they were passive investors. There were no Trust meetings, and there was no regular place of meeting. There were no records and no cash, because they would leave a trail. When a refinery made profits, instead of distributing the profits amongst the shareholders, it turned them over to the sugar trustees. The only books the Trust would keep were a certificate book and a transfer book. The sole paperwork of any kind was memoranda of understanding drawn up by Dos Pasos and kept by Searles, which was regarded as protected by attorney-client privilege.

In the early spring of 1887, the Havemeyers let it be known that they were going to form a sugar refiners Trust. Harry was able to form the trust because all the major sugar refiners recognized him as a true leader. They also believed that he was incapable of any kind of fraud or deception.

Quickly, eight other New York-area firms joined, including Donner and DeCastro of Williamsburg, his cousin Hector Havemeyer, who owned the Greenpoint refinery, Dick and Meyer, who refined right next to Havemeyer and Elder, the Brooklyn Sugar refinery, the Oxnard brothers, the Mathieson refinery in Jersey City and the Weichers family refinery. One key refiner remained outside the Trust, Joseph B. Thomas of Boston, whose Standard Sugar Refining Company could refine 2,700,000 pounds of sugar a day. Searles repeatedly visited Boston, trying to convince him, but his efforts proved fruitless and Thomas remained unconvinced. Finally, Harry offered Lowell Palmer $100,000 if he could convince Thomas to join. After Palmer carefully explained the details of the Trust and allayed his fears, Thomas decided to join and Searles came to Boston to enroll Thomas in the Trust. By the first week in April, most American refiners had entered the scheme. Five Boston refineries, including Thomas, joined the eight New York area firms along with E. C Knight of Philadelphia.

A mercantile committee made up of Harry as chairman, Julius Stursburg, John Jurgensen, Williams Dick, John Searles and John B. Thomas made all the decisions. The Trust acquired some refineries only to shut them down to limit the supply of sugar on the market. Harry Havemeyer explained another reason for acquiring other refineries, "Sometimes we took in refineries to get the brains that were in the concern."

In April of 1887, the Trust was finally set up, and the cartel began operations. One of the first orders business was to determine which plants would run and which would shut down. All the refineries were told to run flat out for sixty days during this test period and the amount of sugar each produced was recorded. Only the most efficient plants would continue. The directors determined that they only needed to operate five plants, one of which was Havemeyer and Elder. The Donner and DeCastro plant on South Fifth Street was dismantled, and the site eventually became home to the Schafer Brewing Company.

The Trust quickly shut down the least efficient

plants, and five to six thousand men were laid off because of the trust. In 1888, the Trust had the capacity to refine 34,000 barrels of sugar, but actually refined just 23, 000 barrels daily. The actions of the Trust also meant that unannounced layoffs would come more frequently, and last longer, because limited production proved profitable to the trust. When the wives of sugar workers heard about the layoffs they cursed management saying, "May God blast and destroy them. I do not know what the little ones will do this winter." A local grocer commented on the impact of the sudden closure of the refinery on the workers and their families, "It will be dreadful. I do not know how they will manage to get food and clothes. Last winter when the Trust closed the refinery the misery was so great that I cannot describe it to you. Children had no shoes and wives and daughters had to work nights in factories." He continued, "Most men have four to nine children each. Some will be driven into beggary."

The Trust was capitalized at $19,500,000 but by March of 1888, there were already $45,000,000 in stock certificates. Each refinery had to file a daily report showing its purchases of raw sugar, meltings, sales and prices. To ensure firms were reporting honestly, an auditor inspected books. If the Trust felt a company was cheating it, the Trust could remove the manager at the end of the year. Because of its huge size, the Trust could bargain for lower prices in a way that no individual refiner could. Sugar growers had to sell on the trust's terms, and within a year it had forced the price of raw sugar down three-quarters of a cent. The Trust was also able to bargain for special low prices from coal companies, and it demanded, and received, special illegal rebates from railroads.

Sugar prices naturally rose because of the limited supply, and the Trust very soon proved to be highly profitable. The Trust quickly reported profits of $70,000 a day. Harry Havemeyer noted that the savings just from stabilizing prices were sufficient to justify the costs involved in consolidating refining. The Trust returned a 10% profit its first year. In 1889, the Trust declared a special dividend of 8%, and in 1891, after paying out dividends, the trust held a surplus of. $7,000,000. Trust investors realized a profit of 200% by 1891, and the price of sugar certificates rose from 70 cents to $126 within two years. The Sugar Trust paid 110% dividends.

Of course, the Trust's profits meant that consumers had to pay much more for sugar. Because of the sharp and sudden rise in the prices of sugar newspapers across the nation began to report on the actions of the Trust, whose opaque dealings and murky structures frustrated investigative journalists. *The New York Times* declared that "Trusts ought to be investigated thoroughly and unsparingly" and *The New York Tribune* opined that the public had the right to know about "their origin and methods, their influence on production and prices and their part in politics." Some politicians also wanted to investigate this new mysterious form of business organization.

Perhaps there was no other place in America as firmly in the grip of the Trusts' tentacles of as the Williamsburg waterfront, where the massive oil and sugar refineries belched out smoke that blackened and fouled the area. A new trust octopus had been born, and now Harry Havemeyer was determined to fight wars to crush the remaining independent sugar refiners, forcing them to submit to the trust's massive power. Havemeyer would soon begin a series of commercial wars to extend his sugar empire across America.

Chapter Eighteen:
Gladiators

Jack McAuliffe was not only the greatest boxer ever to emerge from Williamsburg, but he was also one of only seven men who could every claim that they had never been defeated in the boxing ring. At the height of his career they composed a ditty dedicated to the diminutive McAuliffe, who was known as "the Napoleon of the Ring."

Napoleon, war master, was a terror to his foes,
A general of generals, as everybody knows,
And Jack McAuliffe, lightweight king
Who won many battles
was tagged by his admirers
The Napoleon of the Ring

It was a fitting sobriquet for one
whose clever wits,

were ever on keen alert
to back his fighting mitts.
But unlike Napoleon the great,
our champion never knew
the stigma of defeat,
Jack did not meet his Waterloo.

Years later, Harry Gilmore, who lost a lightweight decision to McAuliffe, summed up what separated McAuliffe from other fighters. Gilmore explained that it was not hard to take a good athlete and make him into a clever boxer, but unless the fighter has the genuine fighting instinct, he could not be molded into a genuine fighting man. McAuliffe, according to Gilmore, fought because he liked fighting, and Gilmore believed that even if McAuliffe had never stepped into the ring, he would have always been a scrapper.

McAuliffe was born in 1866 in Cork, Ireland, and brought to this country at age five. His father had been a cooper in Ireland, but when his father emigrated he joined the cavalry, and he was part of the force sent out too late to save General Custer after the battle of the Little Big Horn. Jack must have inherited the martial spirit from his father. McAuliffe grew up in Bangor, Maine, and although he was a smallish lad, the bigger bullies knew not to tangle with the tough little Irish kid. At age fifteen, he had his first fight against a British sailor ten years his senior, and twenty to thirty pounds bigger than Jack; nevertheless, Jack emerged victorious, and claimed a prize pool of $8 that the British sailors had collected for the winner.

His father moved the family in 1882 to Williamsburg, where every block had a gang led by a child pugilist who fought for the sheer love and adventure of sparring. When Jack arrived, kids were sent by the gangs to inquire about the new kid on the block. Jack sent each home with a fat lip, and eventually a match was arranged with the toughest kid in the neighborhood, the fearsome Paddy Garrity who greatly outweighed Jack. Although Garrity had a gang, they never interfered in his first match against Jack, which was held under a street lamp, and was broken up by the police. The two boys agreed to return to the same spot on North Second Street each night until a champion emerged. Finally, on the seventh night Garrity did not show up, and Jack was proclaimed the child boxing king of Williamsburg. Years later, McAuliffe recalled that he took more abuse from Garrity than he did from professionals in the ring.

McAuliffe entered his father's trade, and was apprenticed in a cooperage on North Fourth Street, learning how to make barrels. It was fate that he would sit on the same bench in the cooperage as another great local fighter, Jack Dempsey, who would soon earn the nickname, the non-pareil, because no one could equal the middleweight in the ring. Dempsey asked McAuliffe one day if he fancied a bit of sparring, thus beginning one of the truly great friendships of early prize fighting history. The two apprentices spent most of their spare time behind freight cars, practicing boxing and the new ideas of footwork and sidestepping in order to become scientific boxers, instead of mere sluggers. Hour after Hour, Dempsey and McAuliffe would work to perfect side-stepping, slipping punches and rolling with a blow so as to take as much of the force off as possible. Dempsey would stand with his back against the wall, and ask Jack to try to hit him with a straight right hand, while he was holding his own hands behind his back. Dempsey soon got so good that all he had to do was bend his head three or four inches and Jack would miss, but soon Jack learned the technique as well, and McAuliffe eventually became as proficient at dodging blows as his sparring partner.

The two boys constantly sparred together, and studied every aspect of the science of boxing, practicing their ring technique in a jerry-rigged ring. They lifted homemade weights, and improvised a punching bag from a canvas sack filled with sawdust and sand. Dempsey was four years older than Jack, and he quickly achieved success in the ring that jack hoped to emulate.

Jack's first amateur fight was a bare-knuckle bout at a Bowery saloon called Harry White's, and his opponent was an older, tougher and heavier lightweight, Jack Mace, a Bowery tough who many regarded as an up-and-coming fighter. Jack's training with Dempsey, who served as his second, paid off. Mace was a brawler who soon proved that he was no match for McAuliffe, who was already a brilliant ring technician who fought tactically. In those days Prize fighting was illegal, but every bar and saloon had a house fighter, a man who would take on all comers in a bare knuckle winner takes all fight. "It was this fight" Jack said, "that gave me the two things every fighter needs, the twin jewels; pride and confidence." By the third round, Jack had his opponent hurt, blood was pouring from Mace's nose, and his eyes were beginning to swell shut, so it was time to finish the job. He laid a right hand on Mace's jaw, who went down for the full count. "It was the first time I had ever seen a man fall unconscious at my feet" Jack would later say, "but I knew it wouldn't be the last; there's an old Irish superstition that fate chooses one specific moment to plot the course of a man's life, that was my moment."

Jack won so many other amateur fights that he issued a challenge to any featherweight to defeat him, and claim a $50 prize. Boxing was still an illegal sport in 1884 when on October 19, an enemy from the same cooperage, Jack Karcher, accepted Jack's challenge. Karcher was an older and bigger boy than the eighteen-year-old Jack who assumed his larger size would prove to be the wining difference.

They arranged to fight the match behind the walls of Evergreen Cemetery so that no police would interfere. The two boxers fought with kid gloves, which soon left both fighters cut up and bleeding. Jack's mobility and ducking proved to be superior, as did his tactics. By the seventeenth round, Karcher was tired, and he dropped his guard when Jack feinted with a left, but hit Karcher with a powerful right to the chin that sent him down to the canvas. The fight had lasted an hour and eight minutes, and marked the end of Jack's amateur career.

McAuliffe would soon fight a legendary title bout. Gem Carney, a British bricklayer with Irish parents who fought out of Birmingham England and had once been tried for killing a man in the ring, came to America to fight McAuliffe. Carney was the British and European Lightweight Champion, and the only man at the time who could dispute McAuliffe's claim as the true light champion of the world. The fight was scheduled to take place in May of 1887, but was canceled because McAuliffe failed to come up with the stake money. It was rescheduled for October, but was once again canceled because Jack had picked up an illness, which severely weakened him. Finally, the fight was signed to take place on the 16th of November in a barn in Westerly Beach, Rhode Island, and would turn out to be one of the most grueling and controversial bouts in boxing history.

The fight began at one o'clock in the morning due to fears of the police. The barn was dimly lit with kerosene lamps that had mirrored reflectors. Each of the boxers wore skintight gloves. In the very first round McAuliffe dropped Carney three times. For the next nine rounds McAuliffe dominated, so much so that in the tenth round, one of Carney's backer's jumped into ring and yelled "Police" to try to stop the fight, but one of Jack's backers named Charley Johnson climbed through the ropes, put his hand on his pistol and exclaimed "I will shoot any man who doesn't get out of the ring immediately." The bout continued, and for the next ten rounds Carney began to come into the fight, slowly wearing Jack down.

In the twenty-sixth round, Carney head-butted Jack in the mid section. which forced him to take a knee, his handlers jumped into the ring and a riot nearly broke out, but one of Carney's backers entered the ring with a drawn revolver, and somehow the referee managed to regain control and the fight continued. Between the twenty-seventh and twenty-eighth rounds while in the corner Dempsey told McAuliffe to "get into a clinch, pull his head over your shoulder and yell that you've been bitten. Jack did just that, and for a brief moment it looked like the referee was going to disqualify Carney, until he opened his mouth and showed he had no front teeth!

The fight continued at a furious pace for the next thirty rounds, with Carney getting much the better of the action until the sixty-second round when McAuliffe produced a brilliant right hand, dropping Carney on his back. The effects of his previous illness were kicking in though, and McAuliffe grew increasingly fatigued. In the seventieth round Carney put McAuliffe down with a left hook, but Jack's handlers jumped into the ring to delay the action, giving their man time to recover. The bout resumed, but in the seventy-fourth round Carney knocked jack down, and once again McAuliffe's handlers entered the ring. A melee ensued, and the man who had staged the fight, fearing a police raid, told the referee Ray Stevenson to end the bout. The referee had decided to end the fight in order to stop a riot from breaking out. He took both men to the center of the ring, and declared the fight a draw. After three hours and forty minutes of a foul-filled war, Jack McAuliffe somehow walked away with his championship intact.

One man who was not impressed by McAuliffe's record and title belt was Sam Collyer, the forty-six year old former Medal of Honor winner and one-time light-weight world champion. When McAuliffe said that he could beat Collyer in a bout, old Sam accepted the challenge of a gloved match in an announcement published by *The Brooklyn Daily Eagle*. At the end of the article, Collyer warned that he meant business.

On December 17, 1888, the two boxers met in the Palace Rink on Grand Street in front of a packed crowd. There was huge excitement because both of the pugilists were local boys and public boxing matches had just become legal. It became apparent that Collyer had grown chunky as he stripped down. The two fighters approached each other in the ring. Collyer appeared serious and worried, while McAuliffe appeared breezy and self-confident. The fight started, and the crowd responded with a huge roar. McAuliffe scored blow after blow, and when Collyer tried to hit him, he avoided the older boxer's blows with ease. Someone yelled out, much to the amusement of the crowd, "What in the devil did you want to get in front of that feller for Sam?" It quickly became apparent that Collyer was no match for Jack in strength, agility or technique, and by the end of the round McAuliffe was seemingly landing punches at will on Collyer.

Collyer looked both shocked and worried in his corner. As the second round started, the two fighters approached each other and threw a few punches, but Jack got inside on Collyer, landing a few hard body blows. Collyer staggered back and dropped his guard momentarily, but that was all the time Jack needed. Pouncing on the opening, McAuliffe threw a powerful right that connected to Collyer's jaw with massive effect. Collyer threw out both arms and staggered back against the ring, collapsing and struggling with unconsciousness. The cruel spectators in the crowd mocked the stricken Collyer, taunting him and crying out, "I told you so." It was the ignominious end of Collyer's once-glorious boxing career.

The Sugar Trust also sought to defeat its adversaries. In 1887, John Searles approached Claus Spreckles, the dominant sugar refiner on the West Coast, to join The Sugar Trust. Spreckles turned him down, saying that his stockholders would have nothing to say in running the business if he joined the Trust. Furthermore, he told Searles that he had come to America from Germany for freedom, and he was determined to maintain his liberty. Havemeyer and the other members of the Trust determined that they had to destroy the independent Spreckles, but the German immigrant would prove to be a tenacious fighter.

Spreckles had immigrated to the United States in 1846, starting as a grocer in Charleston, South Carolina. He spent time in New York before eventually moving to California, where he opened a brewery. Realizing that there were huge untapped profits in sugar refining, he set up the Bay Sugar Refining Company in cooperation with several partners beginning in 1863, and incorporated the business in 1864. Spreckels directed company operations until 1865, and then sold the enterprise, again at a considerable profit, but he had a plan to return to sugar refining. In 1865, he visited Germany to investigate beet-sugar production. Hiding his true identity, he obtained employment in a Magdeburg refinery, most likely Jacob Hennige & Co., while secretly studying the company's secrets of sugar refinement. He learned every aspect of industrial refining, mastering the complex calculus of labor, transport, wholesale trading and export costs in sugar production.

Returning to San Francisco, he built the California Sugar Refinery in 1867, which initially had a capacity of 9,000 tons per year, but Spreckels, using the knowledge he had acquired in Germany, sped the production process up with new machines, some of which he patented. He shortened refining time from three weeks to just twenty-four hours. He also introduced several new sugar products. At that time, grocery stores dominantly sold sugar loaves, but Spreckels introduced granulated and cube sugar, both already well known in Europe, which allowed consumers to more easily divide portions. His sugar was a hit because it had a clean appearance, good quality, and sold at a low price. Spreckels benefited, as well, from the economies of scale—enlarging his buildings on four occasions. Most of his competitors were blown out of the Western market, and only one larger firm survived the completion of his new refinery in 1881—the most modern American facility of the time. Spreckels had become the "Sugar King" of California—and a millionaire.

Spreckles saw that the key to Western sugar refining was controlling the Hawaiian sugar fields. He purchased 40,000 acres on the Island of Maui, erected an impressive system of irrigation canals, and even set up a fleet of steamboats to bring the raw sugar to his refinery. He extended his economic grasp of the market year by year. In 1883, Spreckels purchased the entire

Hawaiian crop of sugar to refine at his San Francisco plant. When he incorporated the Hawaiian Commercial and Sugar Company with $10,000,000 capital in 1884, it included four sugar mills, thirty-five miles of railroad with rolling stock, a water reservoir and the most advanced canal system in the Pacific. Spreckels had created a veritable "sugar empire," which his two eldest sons helped him run, that produced much cheaper sugar than his competitors.

Soon after, the Trust began its "sugar war," and an amazing chapter of American business history commenced. The Sugar Trust purchased Spreckels' former competitor in San Francisco and cut sugar prices, but Spreckles fought back valiantly. "This Trust has trampled on my toes and I won't stand it." He wanted to take his war to the Trust, and he came East with huge cash reserves, intent on building a refinery that would beat the Trust in terms of output and cost. After negotiating with the local authorities in Philadelphia, he invested approximately $4,000,000 to establish the world's largest refinery there, which had access to cheap coal, an abundant water supply, and excellent transport facilities. By the time the refinery started production in 1889 with a capacity of two million pounds per year, Spreckels had become a prominent figure across America in his fight for cheap sugar and private entrepreneurship. The Trust was determined to destroy Spreckles, and even sold sugar at a loss to drive him out of business. Sugar prices dropped dramatically, while Spreckels spread rumors of establishing another refinery in New Orleans.

The Trust proved to be unscrupulous in its war against Spreckles. Agents of the Sugar Trust destroyed parts of Spreckels' machinery, the most significant being the modern vacuum pans, and his sugar was spoiled overnight. Even a chief accountant was bribed to inform the Sugar Trust of orders and finances. At the same time, the Sugar Trust tried to reach an agreement with Spreckels, but he was more interested in his public status as anti-trust hero, and also in the success of his Philadelphia plant: "I came here to fight the Trust, and I have fought it, and I intend to keep on fighting it." However, in March of 1891, people could tell the "sugar war" had ended when the price of refined sugar rose, although both Spreckles and the trust remained mum. The Sugar Trust's California plant was closed, and Spreckels was confirmed as the sugar king of the West. The Sugar Trust bought the Philadelphia refinery for nearly $7 million dollars, running it from 1892 onward. Thereafter, both sides cooperated. Spreckels had supposedly won the "war" because he kept his independence, but critics judged him much more harshly: "This is the man by whose action the Sugar Trust was enabled to complete and perfect its monopoly." His surrender to the Trust meant a doubling in value of his investment, while enabling the Trust to add three-eighths or one-half- a cent to the price of every pound of refined sugar consumed in this country.

Havemeyer and the Trust would fight other wars to maintain the trust's dominance over sugar refining. John and Charles Arbuckle came to Brooklyn from Pittsburgh, and they soon built the largest coffee company in the United States by 1892, selling twice as much coffee as their two nearest competitors combined. Arbuckle Brothers firm was often called, " the coffee trust." Much of their success resulted from the popular paper bags the brothers packaged their coffee in. Their machines filled a conveyor belt of paper bags with sixteen ounces of ground, mechanically sealed coffee. The brothers had wisely purchased the bagging machine from its inventor.

One day, they realized that they could use the bagging machine to package and sell sugar, which they purchased from the Trust. Soon they were bagging 250,000 pounds of sugar a year, because consumers thought bagged sugar was cleaner than sugar scooped by a merchant from a barrel. As a huge customer, Arbuckle tried to cut a deal with the Trust, given the astronomical quantities they used, but Henry O. Havemeyer felt threatened by Arbuckle's dominant position in the market, and the sugar king refused to cooperate with the Arbuckle firm. The Sugar Trust refused to repurchase empty sugar barrels at twenty cents a barrel, even though the Arbuckle concern was a major purchaser of sugar. Arbuckle also questioned why the price of refined sugar sold by Havemeyer stayed high when the price of raw sugar fell, arousing the ire of Harry Havemeyer.

Franz Matthiessen of the Trust tried to purchase the patent to the bagger from the brothers, but they were too wise to sell it. Havemeyer decided that he would use the power of the trust to drive the Arbuckle brothers into bankruptcy, and then acquire the coveted bagger. Harry was warned that a war with the coffee magnates would hurt his business, but he replied, "Let them start it. They can't hire any sugar talent and even if they did I would put them out of business."

Havemeyer took many aggressive steps to bring the war to the Arbuckles. First, he raised the price of sugar the Trust charged the Arbuckles for wholesale sugar, and then the Trust purchased the Woolson Spice Company, a coffee firm, with the intention of entering the coffee business. Harry entered his war with the

Arbuckles with "all the enthusiasm of a schoolboy." Furious at the attempt to destroy his business, John Arbuckle announced in 1896 his plan to build his own Brooklyn sugar refinery to compete with the Trust. He shrewdly hired the best technical expert on sugar refining, J. F. Stillman, to design and run his plant, and the war was on. A cutting-edge plant full of electrical devices, the refinery could produce 3,000 barrels of sugar per day, much of which would be packaged in retail-sized two-pound paper bags that proved very popular with consumers. In 1898, the Arbuckle refinery in Dumbo could only produce a quarter of what a trust refinery could generate, but it led to a sugar war, with the price of sugar soon dropping five cents per pound. The Arbuckle refinery could compete with the trust because it was technologically more up to date. The opening of the new plant pushed the margin on sugar refining to a half cent a pound, forcing the Trust to sell sugar at a loss.

Letting Skillman leave and work for his rivals hurt Havemeyer in many ways. Skillman had no peer in terms of merchandising and technological skills. Skillman did not use a buyer to select his sugar; he knew exactly the type of sugar the company should refine, which he selected on the basis of taste and not price. He produced handsome soft sugar, which tasted far better than the Eagle brand of sugar Havemeyer and Elder considered to be the gold standard in American refined sugar.

Another firm decided to enter the sugar refining business. In 1898, one of the founding members of the Trust, Claus Doscher, re-entered the sugar market and set up the New York Sugar Refinery Company in Long Island City. By November of that year, his firm was turning out 3,000 barrels of sugar a day. Doscher had been one of the original founders of the sugar trust as president of the Brooklyn Sugar Refining Company. His entry into the market infuriated Harry Havemeyer who considered it an act of betrayal. Harry fired Doscher's sons who worked in the Havemeyer and Elder plant in revenge. Harry also vowed to destroy Doscher.

Harry was determined to prevent the Arbuckles from selling to wholesalers, whom he threatened with loss of access to his sugar if they sold the sugar of any competitor. The Arbuckles had trouble finding any wholesalers, but they succeeded by selling some sugar to retailers directly. The price war was hurting the Arbuckles, who privately admitted that they had lost $1,225,000 in the sugar refining business, but they were as independent of mind, and as fiercely competitive, as Harry Havemeyer, so they remained in the sugar refining game.

Harry also began to sell his coffee at a loss, the price dropping to ten cents, twelve cents cheaper than a decade previously, but the "Sugar King" was determined to destroy his rivals. John Arbuckle remained adamant, vowing that the coffee price cut would not drive him out of the sugar refining business. Soon both Woolson and Arbuckle were losing millions, but each was determined to emerge victorious from the coffee price war. Havemeyer in 1899 attacked on another coffee front, opening the American Coffee Company in a former sugar refinery in Williamsburg. The plant took up an entire city block, and with twenty-two roasting machines it was the largest coffee-roasting firm in America.

The war was severely damaging both the Trust and the Arbuckle firm. The market share of the Trust fell to 80% and the company had to dip into its reserves to pay dividends. The reduced profits led to a drop in the share price of Trust stock. The "war" lasted several years. Arbuckle had the industrial facilities to refine his sugar, and a sales organization already in place to market it. His refinery soon upped its production to 5,000 barrels a day. While Harry Havemayer was away in Europe, trustee Lowell Palmer sat down with John Arbuckle and other trust directors because he could see how much the war was costing both sides. He reached an agreement with Arbuckle to end the war. When Harry returned from Europe and learned about the agreement, he grew furious. He took the paper the agreement was signed on, tore it up and stomped on it, stating that he would never enter into an agreement with those men, but instead would drive them out of business. The disagreement led to the beginning of fallout between Havemeyer and Palmer.

In the end Havemeyer folded, and left the coffee business. In January 1901, the two sides negotiated an end to the war, which had cost them an estimated $25,000,000. The two giants must have agreed to a truce because the price of sugar suddenly rose, but they were smart enough to leave no incriminating documents. Havemeyer's attempts to destroy his competitors would soon lead to a rival's suicide, criminal indictments and a national scandal.

Chapter Nineteen:
Trustworthy Politicians?

Harry Havemeyer understood that he could not hold and further consolidate his empire if he did not make friends with lawmakers in Albany and, more importantly, in Washington. Politicians faced pressure to act against the Trust from newspapers, which noted that trust member John Searles earned the same salary as the president of the United States, and observed that if the Trust lasted ten more years Harry would be the richest man in the country. They also reported that in a year Havemeyer's wealth went from $15,000 to $50,000,000.

Harry, however, did not fear the papers, nor did he doubt his ability to advance the Trust's agenda in both capitals because he believed that politicians could be bought just as readily as any business or commodity could be purchased, and no other man in America had been so bold and unscrupulous in testing this theory amongst lawmakers on the state and national level. Havemeyer considered government an adjunct to business. He believed he could utilize government to make money, and then use that money to corrupt government into giving him more favors that would make him still more money with which to further corrupt government.

Harry and the Trust proved wily in fighting anti-trust laws and judicial decisions. In 1888, the court dealt a blow to the Trust, but Havemeyer and his legions of corporate lawyers proved well able to surmount the legal challenges mounted against it. In 1888, New York State's attorney general brought suit against North River Sugar refining Company part of the Trust, claiming that the Trust was assuming corporate powers without being incorporated in New York State.

The Trust obviously bought the best legal talent in the country to defend its position, but lost anyway. In 1889 the New York State Supreme Court said that the combination made by the Trust was in fact a monopoly. It also ruled that a corporation could not surrender entire control of its franchise to another body. Moreover, The Trust's charter in New York State was annulled, and the court held that the Trust was, in fact, a virtual conspiracy to hold up prices and stifle competition. The decision was a resounding blow against Havemeyer and his associates, but the Trust's lawyers simply moved the conglomerate to New Jersey, where it was re-chartered under New Jersey law, which allowed holding companies to exist. The Sugar Trust reorganized as a holding company, the American Sugar Refining Company, which was incorporated in New Jersey on January 10, 1891, by attorneys Elihu Root and John Randolph Dos Passos. Effectively, the business practices of the American Sugar Refining Company exactly replicated those of the Sugar Refineries Company, and the firm even continued to be known as the Sugar Trust.

There was a more serious challenge to the Trust on the national level in the form of legislation passed by Congress and signed into law in 1890 called the Sherman Anti-Trust act, under which federal prosecutors could have sued to break up the trust as a monopoly. However, the wording of the Sherman Antitrust Act was ambiguous and the act failed to define such key terms as "trust," "conspiracy," "restraint of trade or commerce," "monopolize," or "combine." As a result, the U.S. courts struggled throughout the 1890s to give precise legal meaning to the law. The trust had little to fear from prosecution by the pro-business Harrison administration, to whose campaign the trust had contributed heavily.

The Harrison administration gifted the Sugar Trust several million dollars when it removed all import duties on raw sugar under the McKinley Tariff of 1890. The removal of the tariff was a huge victory for the Trust in its war with Claus Spreckles, and it was part of the reason that Spreckles gave up his fight against the trust and sold out to the Trust. Furthermore, the McKinley Tariff helped the Trust by erecting a duty on foreign refined sugar that shielded it from foreign competition, and allowed it to charge high prices without fear of foreign competitors who could drive down the price the consumer paid for refined sugar. The Harrison years were a golden era for the Trust, and the Trust was determined to use its power and financial influence to maintain the status quo when the next administration took power.

In 1892, Grover Cleveland, a Democrat, ran for president on a pledge to the American consumer to restore free trade and to end protective tariffs that made goods more expensive to them. Havemeyer also was afraid that the new administration might impose a duty on raw imported sugar. Havemeyer feared that new tariff laws might deprive him of the funds he needed to wage his economic wars with his competitors. Havemeyer, though, planned to buy the Democrats, and dismantle their free trade agenda in relation to sugar. For the 1892 campaign, the Sugar Trust gave the Democratic Party candidate Grover Cleveland $500,000, and Havemeyer had a secret personal meeting with the presidential candidate on Havemeyer's private yacht. The Trust made a huge campaign contribution just in time to save several imperiled states for the Democrats and help them to secure the election. Several Democrats repaid the favor by helping to advocate for a tariff favorable to the Trust.

When Cleveland was elected, he named a personal friend of Havemeyer, John G. Carlisle, as Secretary of the Treasury who gave Harry letters of introduction to key Democratic senators who sat on the Finance Committee that would decide the question of the sugar tariff. Louisiana senators, in particular, wanted to tax raw imported sugar to protect their state's sugar industry. Searles and Havemeyer realized that they would lose their duty-free sugar imports, and had to accept some tariff. They compromised and accepted an ad valorum, or value-based tax, because it was cheaper than a one-cent tax on raw sugar across the board. Many Democrats advocated a one cent-across-the-board tax on raw sugar that would have cost the trust millions.

In 1894, while the tariff question was being debated, Havemeyer took a room in the Arlington Hotel in Washington where he had a series of private meetings with those Democratic Senators. When it was time to draw up the sugar tariff schedule, the Secretary of the Treasury took notes in his own hand just as Havemeyer dictated it to him. Carlisle also made an impassioned plea to the Finance Committee to help his personal friend and the Trust, stating:

> Gentlemen there is one thing I am bound to say to you as earnestly and impressively as I can do it and I speak to you as a Democrat to Democrats. No party, or the representatives of no party can afford to ignore honorable obligations. I want to say to you that there seems to be a danger that this is going to be done. Gentlemen associated with the sugar refining interests subscribed to the campaign fund of the Democratic Party in 1892 a very large sum of money. They contributed several thousand dollars at a time when we urgently needed it. I tell you that it would be wrong, it would be infamous, after having accepted that important contribution, given at a time when it was imperatively needed for the Democratic Party to turn around and strike down the men who gave it. I trust you will prepare an amendment to the bill, which will be reasonable and in

some measure satisfactory to those interests.

Havemeyer did not come to Washington alone, bringing with him an army of lobbyists and agents who swarmed the capital. It was the largest and most brazen lobbying effort Washington had yet seen. Havemeyer explained to the senators how they could get rich through stock speculation. If they agreed to a favorable tariff, then they could make money by buying stock at a lower price and selling at a higher price, after they voted for a lower sugar tariff. Havemeyer himself that year made more in stock speculation than he did refining sugar, a fact that he must have shared with the senators on the Finance committee. Many senators were tempted by the chance to make such easy money, and some actually purchased trust stock, expecting a windfall. The newspapers reported that the Trust was bribing senators, which led to outrage in Washington and many denials. However, Senator Quay of Pennsylvania brazenly admitted buying sugar stock: "Certainly, I have been speculating in sugar. Why not?" Senator Aldrich of Rhode Island was so vehement in advocating for the Trust that he earned the sobriquet, "The Sugar Senator."

Havemeyer and the Trust won the ad valorum tariff, which became a national scandal. Trust stock went from eight to fourteen on the day that the favorable amendments to the sugar industry were made, enriching senators who had speculated in the stock. President Cleveland called the pro-trust tariff revision "national perfidy," and said that the men who enacted it should never be forgiven or forgotten, so he refused to sign the bill, at first, but it eventually became law.

Public outrage over the bribing of senators and the power of the sugar lobby led to the creation of a special senate committee to investigate the scandal. Sugar Trust agents, however, faced the committee with snarling defiance, stoking more public outrage. Everton Chapman, a stockbroker who was called in front of the committee to testify on senators who bought sugar stock, defied the committee, refusing to name the senators and was convicted of, and served time for contempt.

Havemeyer was equally brazen in his testimony, and showed himself to be highly contemptuous of the committee. He publically admitted controlling the price of sugar in the senate. Harry also stated that he thought it justified to get all he could out of the consumer. He said, "I do not care two cents for your ethics, and I do not know enough of them to apply them," when asked about the morality of buying votes.

Havemeyer also told federal investigators that

it was his company's policy to maintain and protect trade, even if it resulted in crushing a competitor he did not care. In his testimony Havemeyer took the position that he gave all the info that the law required, and would give only as much as the stockholders instructed him to give, but he would publish nothing that would help his competitors. He was so uncooperative that he was put on trial for contempt of the senate, but the charges were later dropped. Harry left Washington proving the power of the Trust's money to determine important public legislation, and to frustrate the public interest.

Harry proved himself to be a master of spin in his Senate testimony. He claimed that the formation of the Trust was the result of the government's unfair raw sugar trade duties, saying, "The mother of all trusts is the customs tariff." Harry also claimed that the sugar tariff was a "hunger tax" that hurt America's poor, and added to the financial burden the poorest Americans faced. He even claimed that every man, woman and child in the United States was directly interested in getting rid of the tariff, and amazingly Harry presented himself as a champion of the American consumer.

The Trust got a further benefit from the Supreme Court, which allowed it to function as a monopoly. In the United States v. E. C. Knight (1895), the Supreme

Court ruled on the Sherman Antitrust Act, which stated that "every person who shall monopolize, or attempt to monopolize, or combine or conspire with any other person or persons, to monopolize any part of the trade or commerce among the several States … shall be deemed guilty of a felony." Not long after the Sherman Act became law, the Trust bought out four other sugar refineries, increasing its control over national sugar production to 98%. In response, the U.S. government sought to invalidate American Sugar's purchase in a lower federal court on the grounds that it violated the Sherman Act. The lower court dismissed the case, and the government appealed to the Supreme Court. In an 8-1 decision written by Chief Justice Melville W. Fuller, the Court ruled that the government lacked power under the Constitution to enforce the Sherman Act against the company's manufacturing operations. Congress' powers are limited to those enumerated in the Constitution, the Court argued, and only one of those powers, that given by the Constitution's Commerce Clause, allow Congress to "regulate commerce … among the several States." Manufacturing operations are not "interstate commerce," the Court asserted, because such operations occur entirely in one state. In short, Congress has the power to regulate trade, but not manufacturing.

Havemeyer not only wanted the government to give the Trust favorable tariffs, but he also wanted it to wrest the main sources of raw sugar, Cuba and Puerto Rico, away from Spain so that the trust and other American investors could create economies in those islands that would be totally dependent on American sugar exports.

Fully half of the refined sugar in America in the 1880s was grown in Cuba, so the stakes were huge. Though nominally controlled by Spain, Cuba was already by the 1880s an American economic colony. Ramon O. Williams, the U.S. consul to Havana, reported in a dispatch of Dec. 28, 1886 "*de facto*, Cuba is already inside the commercial union of the United States. The whole commercial machinery of Cuba depends upon the sugar market of the United States."

Havemeyer's holding company, the Cuban American Sugar Company, already owned up to a third of the Cuban sugar crop before the declaration of the 1898 Spanish American War, which was sometimes called "Havemeyer's War" because there were few Americans who were so jingoistic in their support of the war as Harry. The press described the conflict not as an economic struggle of American industry to gain control over a vital resource, but as assistance to an oppressed people fighting to gain their freedom.

Puerto Rico became a United States territory as a result of the 1898 war, but the most important change was not governmental but economic as the Puerto Rican economy was transformed to make it a virtual sugar-producing American colony. From 1899 to 1909, there was a tenfold increase in the amount of sugar the island produced. Its ports, roads, railroads and most of its transportation infrastructure were built to facilitate the movement of its sugar northwards.

Cuba was treated in a similar way. The Trust, with the huge influence that it yielded in Washington, determined Cuba's status not in relation to the wishes of her people, but as the Trust's most important sugar producing colony. There was talk of annexing Cuba, but the Trust opposed it because admitting Cuba as a state could benefit Havemeyer's competition. Other refiners could set up Cuban refineries that would be able to undercut the Trust's competitive cost advantages. Harry knew that Cuban admission would mean disaster for him. The life of the Trust depended on keeping out all refined sugar, and giving the Trust special raw sugar import privileges. He prevented Cuba from becoming an American territory, and then proceeded to subjugate it. By 1903, Henry Havemayer controlled, directly or indirectly, the entire Cuban sugar crop. After gaining control of Cuba, Havemeyer could set the price of raw sugar too.

By 1903, though, the sugar market had changed, but the wily Havemeyer was again one step ahead of the game. Western farmers proved that they could grow large crops of commercially viable beet sugar, and the prospect loomed of sugar being a domestic, not an imported commodity. In 1901, Havemeyer realized that American-grown beet sugar was viable commercially and, of course, the Trust planned to dominate the production of beet sugar as well. The Trust increased its capitalization from $75,000,000 to $90,000,000 to buy up the beet sugar industry. In the same year the Trust cut the price of sugar three and a half cents in the beet sugar market areas at the very time when beet sugar was first coming to market. Havemeyer was also able to use illegal railroad rebates to ship huge quantities of sugar, and store it in beet-producing areas at almost no cost. Suddenly, the price of sugar dropped below cost and beet sugar men simply could not sell their sugar at a profit. They faced financial ruin. Beet sugar men, unable to compete, had to sell out to Havemeyer.

In Late 1902, the Trust entered into contract with the American Beet Sugar Company to be agent for sales of Beet sugar, agreeing to a quarter-cent-a-pound commission. In 1903, Havemeyer's American Sugar

Refining Company started to buy up beet sugar firms. American's Board of Directors appointed a committee to take charge of the purchasing and management of beet sugar companies. Soon, the Trust had a growing portfolio of beet sugar. Havemeyer soon cornered the beet sugar market by buying up stock in beet sugar companies. Buying up the beet sugar industry kept it from becoming a threat to his monopoly over the sugar crop.

With a huge stake in the beet sugar market, Havemeyer was ready to raise the tariff on imported sugar because it would raise the price of raw sugar in the world market and mean another windfall for the trust, but first Havemeyer wanted to manipulate the market even further. In 1901 and 1902, the Trust began to hoard sugar, and created an artificial shortage in the sugar market. The Trust's warehouses were full to capacity with imported Cuban sugar, but it sat in storage instead of being sold in the sugar-hungry marketplace.

The hoarding of sugar was part of a devious Havemeyer plan. In 1903, American lawmakers were clamoring for a revision of the tariff laws to protect the nascent American beet-sugar industry. The Trust realized that its opposition to a higher tariff would be futile, but it also was in a position to reap profits from a tariff increase thanks to its dominance of domestic beet sugar production. The 20% sugar duty enacted in 1903 became a windfall for Havemeyer and the Trust because he had hoarded sugar, storing tons of it in warehouses. When the tariff came into effect it increased the price of sugar, making his hoarded stockpile more valuable and the Trust's beet-sugar holdings.

If the federal government was proving feckless in its defense of sugar workers and consumers, then local, city and state elected officials in Brooklyn were not only equally as negligent, but even more so. For many years, Brooklyn had been run by a cartel that was every bit as corrupt, rapacious and lawless as the Sugar Trust. The corrupt Democratic Party machine that ran Brooklyn was known as "the Ring," and its leader was one of the most effective and long-lasting political bosses, Hugh McLaughlin, who ran the city of Brooklyn as despotically as any Czar ever ran Russia.

Hugh McLaughlin reigned as a power behind the throne, running Brooklyn for almost forty years as its political boss. Thoroughly corrupt, McLaughlin became a millionaire through kickbacks, sweetheart deals and insider real estate speculation among many other forms of corruption. For decades, nothing happened in Brooklyn city government without the consent of McLaughlin.

The son of Irish immigrants, McLaughlin started life as a fishmonger and street thug who became a protégé of the mayor of Brooklyn, Henry Murphy, who rewarded him with a position as a master mechanic in the Brooklyn Navy Yard that gave McLaughlin control over hiring there. McLaughlin used the Navy Yard job to build a web of patronage, which he soon parleyed into political power. In 1862, he became the boss of "the Ring". As such, he dominated local politics for many years, despite the efforts of reform-oriented mayors like Frederick A. Schroeder and Seth Low to roll back the influence of the Brooklyn Ring.

McLaughlin chose all of the candidates selected by the Democratic Party of Brooklyn, and his absolute power in Brooklyn stemmed from this ability to nominate all of the important officials, who were beholden to him and served at his pleasure. McLaughlin could end a man's political career at will by deciding to ostracize him, so McLaughlin could make or break any potential candidate's chances. Running the ring required strict discipline, and McLaughlin never forgot or forgave even the smallest offenses. Office holders knew that if they disobeyed the boss they had no political future. *The New York Tribune* gave a synopsis of how he ruled Brooklyn.

McLaughlin names the mayor. The mayor reap-
points the boss's men to fill departments with Democratic place hunters. The office holders raid a boodle for the re-election of the boss's candidate for
mayor and the boodle is used in hiring naturalized
citizens ground out on Judge Moon's court to vote
for the boss' ticket and in employing repeaters to
violate the election law and so is the circle of the
ring's iniquity squared.

In 1873, McLaughlin retired from his official position as Brooklyn City Registrar because he was making far more money running the Ring. The boss chose
his lieutenants carefully because they could expose
the massive corruption that was the lifeblood of the
ring. McLaughlin was able to hold power for so long
because he co-opted many of the best and brightest
young politicians in Brooklyn. He picked young men
of ability and gave them a minor position, watching to
see if they merited a higher position in the Ring.

Blind loyalty to McLaughlin and unquestioning
obedience to the Ring, were paramount virtues in the
eyes of the boss. Underlings had to support his every
effort at crushing reform and hiding corruption. The
expression of honest convictions could mean polit-

ical suicide, and the boss considered the exercise of individual judgment treason. Men were motivated to blindly follow the boss by a share in the spoils. John Shelvin, his errand boy, became wealthy by overcharging the city on the no-bid contracts he received. His lieutenant, John Kingsley, became rich through paving contracts, and the entire inner circle was also rewarded.

McLaughlin held court at Kerrigan's Auction House on Willoughby Street. Everyone had to go there for favors, but one of the most common was at the time of death, for McLaughlin won votes by paying for the funerals of the Irish poor. The boss was a corpulent, round-faced man with small, keen blue eyes. A six-footer with big shoulders and a potbelly, McLaughlin reminded some of a well-to-do Irish squire with a double chin, fat cheeks and an inscrutable poker face. He hated open conflict, but enjoyed receiving guests who kowtowed to his vast influence and power.

McLaughlin tabbed McCarren at an early age to enter the ring. At age twenty-one, McCarren was elected to the party committee, and in his early twenties he became a member of the ward committee. It was said that he knew every man, woman and child in the ward, most of whom owed him a vote because McCarren had helped them in some way.

McCarren had dreams of wielding power far beyond his Williamsburg ward. McCarren compensated for his lack of formal education by studying oratory, and he became one of the most effective speakers in Brooklyn, who often made stump speeches in support of ring candidates. He avoided flowery language, but studied up on topics to sound knowledgeable. His favorite expression became "Let's get down to cases."

In 1881, McLaughlin tapped him to run for the State Assembly. He was elected and he quickly joined an infamous group of corrupt lawmakers known as "the Black Horse Cavalry." The Cavalry was a bipartisan group of lawmakers who collected annual fees to block certain pieces of legislation, most of which were injurious to large corporations like the sugar trust or Standard Oil. It was a form of legislative blackmail that enriched lawmakers. Each year, the Cavalry killed fifty to seventy five bills that benefited shrouded interests whose money spoke. The process was so well organized that a single law firm acting for those who contracted the Cavalry's services paid off all the cavalrymen after each session. Manhattan Democrat "Little Tim" Sullivan was almost the king of the Cavalrymen after each legislative session. McCarren also saw that the most effective work was done on committees and not on floor. He avoided speaking on the floor, considering it a waste of effort, but rather focused on getting nominated for key committees, especially ones that could influence the Sugar Trust or Standard Oil.

In 1883, McCarren was re-elected to the legislature, but death struck him when his wife suddenly passed away. She had also born him five children who all died as infants, preceding her to the grave. The death of his wife and kids changed him drastically. He was no longer the genial, big-hearted Pat McCarren who drifted into politics. Some said that he had grown cold, taciturn and disdainful. Afterwards he was a changed man; he showed little or no sentiment, and he became even more driven.

McCarren immersed himself in study. An intellect, he was most interested in how great men made decisions at crucial moments in history. He also decided to become a lawyer, and spent hours and hours in the state library at Albany, preparing himself to pass the bar. He understood that money paid to a politician was a bribe, but money paid to a lawyer was a consultation or a retainer. His goal was to become a lawyer for the trusts in his district, and to become wealthy from their huge profits.

McCarren soon became one of the first corporate lobbyists in American history. He obtained a law degree, but he saw himself first and foremost as a politician. He said, "I do not pretend to know the law. It is true that I am a lawyer, but that is not my business. I am a politician. Every man has to have a sideline. The law is mine. When I want real up-to-date law I go to one of my friends who makes it his business." McCarren quickly proved to be a natural law maker, and he quickly became a leader in the Democratic caucus.

McLaughlin and the machine saw that he would thrive in the senate, and nominated him to represent Williamsburg in the Senate. In 1886, he was elected, and no one proved to be more effective. Even though Democrats were in the minority, he got many bills signed into law. A master horse trader and dealmaker, no one, not even his enemies, denied that he was a master politician. He was a great debater, but he soon realized more was done behind the scenes than on the floor of the senate, so he said little. An astute parliamentarian, he knew how to get opponents to support even the most politically unpopular bills. He stated, "Legislation is a matter of having enough votes. A majority of one is enough. Give me that majority, and I will do whatever I please in either house." A man of his word, he was quite adept at crossing the aisles to make political alliances. McCarren excelled at supporting other people's bills and collecting favors. He once told Senator Foelker, a Brooklyn Republican,

"You need not fear the indignation of your constituents. If you are afraid of possible re-election or have any doubts at election time, I can fix it up for you so that you can name your own opponent at the coming election."

McCarren soon gained a reputation as an extremely confident, but self-serving lawmaker who would sell his services to the highest bidder. He quickly abandoned any pretense of serving the thousands of refinery workers whom he represented, and became a faithful, well-paid acolyte of the trusts. Working for the trusts, he would achieve an unimaginable level of power and wealth. His enemies would accuse him of selling his constituents our and called him " the Sugar Senator."

Chapter Twenty:
The Cynical State Senator Takes Control

In the fall of 1893, Patrick McCarren was the most powerful politician in Williamsburg, and the Corrupt Brooklyn Ring's legislative genius. He shamelessly represented the interests of the trusts, saloon owners and gamblers in Albany. Those interests had rewarded his support by helping him become chairman of the New York Democratic Party State Committee, which gave him huge clout on the state level. While other politicians tried to hide their support of these unpopular groups, McCarren openly supported them and their interests. No other leader in Albany had the courage to champion these cause so openly, while sneering at measures intended to benefit the people. His claims of representing the people of his district were the height of hypocrisy. He was openly a lobbyist for the trusts and worked hand-in-glove with his Republican colleagues to protect them and their interests. Because of his position as Chairman of the State Democratic Committee, he could promise Republicans who supported his bills that they could even name their Democratic opponents in their districts. His corporate clients paid him handsomely for his services, and because of McCarren's influence they had nothing to fear from reform-minded lawmakers.

McCarren, though, had to hide his lobbying for the trusts from his constituents, because the Standard Oil and The Sugar Trust exploited many of them. In 1898, Republican Robert Griffith ran against McCarren for his senate seat, and wanted to make the incumbent's cozy relationship with big business the campaign's central issue. Griffiths printed a damaging circular identifying McCarren as a supporter of the Sugar Trust and the Standard Oil Corporation. When one of Mc-Carren's supporters showed the senator the circular he became furious, realizing its potential for damage. McCarren had previously used the police to win elections, and now he called the police again, demanding that they suppress the circulars. Acting on McCarren's orders, police Captain John Reardon had his men confiscate the Anti-McCarren circulars, while threatening to arrest those who distributed them.

When he learned of the police's role in suppressing his circulars, Griffiths brought the matter to *The*

New York Times, which published the material McCarren wanted suppressed. The circular asked, "Is McCarren owned by Croker, Rockefeller, Havemeyer, Whitney and Flower? He always votes in their interest." It also said, "McCarren always votes in the interest of the Sugar Trust, and is a Democrat for sugar only." The flier also told voters, "Send Griffiths in his (McCarren's) place to vote for you. You might as well vote for one of Havemeyer's sugar barrels as vote for McCarren." Griffiths also quipped in his flier, "McCarren is sugar coated, but is still too bitter a pill for Democrats to swallow." The circular also told voters, "McCarren's pipeline runs through Havemeyer's sugar factory to the Standard Oil Company works. A vote for Griffiths will stop the flow of the mingled oil and sugar in McCarren's ward," and, "Oil and water don't mix, but oil sugar and McCarren do and are entirely too thick. Thin the mixture by turning down McCarren by a vote for anti-trust Griffiths." Possibly the most clever attack on McCarren was a stanza of poetry, "Down with sugar coated Pat. He is not a Democrat. Vote for Griffiths, turn Pat down. Do McCarren nice and brown."

Despite the damaging attacks in the circular, McCarren still won the election. He could thank the Democratic machine for his victory. It provided jobs and did political favors in return for votes. McCarren opened a club in 1891 at 186 Bedford Avenue. The club had seven hundred members. Men who needed work came there to see McCarren, who would often direct them across the street to a Paddy Loftus' bar where they were hired by the police and fire departments and other city agencies. McCarren could also use his influence with the Sugar Trust and Standard Oil to get jobs in their refineries. Each year the Seymour Club hosted an outing for all of its members, hiring a steam ship that sailed to a park where free food and beer were served. The guests got the chance to rub shoulders with elected officials, and even to shake McCarren's hand themselves. At election time, the club's hundreds of members turned into a massive get-out-the-vote operation. The club's support made challenging McCarren seemingly impossible.

By 1893, though, disgust with the corrupt McLaughlin Ring that had put McCarren in power, was growing. An October 1893 *New York Times* expose on the Ring reported on the "shameful misrule" of Brooklyn and identified McCarren as one of the "real rulers" of Brooklyn who had acquired a fortune of $100,000, "not by years of honest toil or by reputable business." The article concluded by saying, "The overburdened tax payers of Brooklyn cannot fail to agree with the visiting French journalist, Rayomond L'Epee, 'A more incredible body of rulers has never been assembled in history. The government of Brooklyn is such as one might expect to see if an archdiocese were run by a horde of Algerine pirates. ' "

The Democratic Party's Brooklyn Ring sickened even honest Democrats with its blatantly corrupt election funding. The papers reported cops were charged $10 for their jobs. Saloonkeepers were threatened with losing their licenses if they did not contribute to the Party. The Democrats had rolled up huge numbers in 1891, and elected their entire county ticket. Taking their electoral mandate as a license to plunder Brooklyn, the Ring began enriching itself shamelessly, while ignoring the fact that taxes were twice as high as in Manhattan, or that the Ring had run up a staggering debt. Brooklyn's debt was so close to its credit limit that no money could be obtained for necessities such as schools, sewers and paving roads.

The mayor of Brooklyn, David Booty, was so beholden to the McLaughlin and the Ring for his election that he did nothing to stop the deprivations of the ring. All his important decisions were determined by party politics, not by the needs of Brooklyn. Booty re-appointed all ex-Mayor Chapin's corrupt commissioners. By re-appointing the men whom he found in office, he proclaimed to Brooklyn and to the world in unmistakable terms, his subservience to the McLaughlin Ring. The mayor gave away valuable railroad franchises for a fraction of what they were worth to men in cahoots with the Ring. No system of civil service functioned in Brooklyn. Jobs were given merely as rewards for loyalty to the Ring. The City Board of Works had the largest payroll and the greatest opportunity to reward loyal contractors with sweetheart deals. It was one of the most corrupt branches of city government, and its corrupt deals cost Brooklyn millions.

There was an outcry all around Brooklyn as people watched in horror as the city was being plundered. A comic in *The World* showed McLaughlin leading an orchestra while members of the Ring danced around Booty. Former Brooklyn Mayor Set Low said of Booty, "The gulls do not follow in the track of an ocean steamer more certainly and more persistently than the schemers and plunderers of Brooklyn beset the pathway of the present mayor." Minister McClellan, a popular Brooklyn preacher, summed up how many honest citizens felt: "Brooklyn is run by a demagogue who administers the affairs of the city not for the benefit of our citizens or for the benefit of the masses, but for the personal pecuniary aggrandizement of those who are in league with him or are henchmen and associates of his associations." Another minister said,

"Brooklyn was not unlike Persia where McLaughlin was the morach and gamblers, saloon keepers and patrons of the prize ring are satraps."

The most notorious member of the Ring finally went too far. Hugh McKane started out as a building contractor in Gravesend, Brooklyn. He soon realized that political influence would greatly benefit his construction business, allowing him to obtain permits that others could not, rezone areas, hold up projects with red tape unless they used his company, and be in the thick of every major construction decision. By the late 1870s, McKane had worked his way up to Gravesend town Supervisor. In the autumn of 1893, there were mayoral elections. Although McKane was a Republican, he had made a corrupt deal with the Ring to back the Democrats. McKane had aroused suspicions because Gravesend had 6,218 registered, while its population was only 8,414. When people came to investigate voter registration they were beaten up or arrested. Brooklyn Republicans decided they needed the law on their side.

The night of the election, as returns were being counted, several carriages filled with Republican Party officials from Brooklyn arrived at the closed Gravesend Town Hall, where McKane and his police confronted them. The newcomers were no ordinary folks, but some of the most socially prominent people of Brooklyn, led by Colonel Alexander S. Bacon. When McKane asked them why they were there, Bacon said that they had come to be watchers for the Republican Party on election day. McKane responded that the full quota of watchers had been assigned by the local Republican Party, telling them to go home. Bacon, producing an injunction, warned McKane that he would be violating the law if he prevented Republican watchers from challenging voters, and from guarding ballot boxes. Famously, McKane replied, "Injunctions don't go here!" A fracas ensued, with McKane's police clubbing some of the intruders and arresting them for drunkenness and disorderly conduct. McKane released them from jail after the election.

McKane's actions were reported in the papers with horror. A journalist for the *Eagle* wrote of McKane:

> He has announced his determination to let none but his gang witness or take past in the election, as he calls what is going on today. He has not only not been interfered with, but also supported by the machine authorities and the sheriff's office of this county, which had been in thorough sympathy with him, and which has not lifted a hand to sustain the courts whose servant the sheriff's office is. This is

civil war. It is successful rebellion. It is treason triumphant."

Even though ordinary people were turning against the Ring, no one wanted to run against Patrick McCarren because of the powerful forces aligned behind him. McCarren's future trajectory seemed upwards. On January 17, 1892, *The New York Times* reported on McCarren's bright political future, claiming that his appointment as the head of the Commerce and Navigation State Senate Committee would allow him to lead the fight to build a second bridge across the East River. The report also said that the people of Brooklyn viewed his appointment as proof that a bill to build a Williamsburg Bridge would pass the Senate, and it told its readers that if the Democrats succeed in getting the bridge bill passed they could make huge inroads into Williamsburg's Republican vote. The *Times* also stated that the party that succeeded in building the span would hold Williamsburg and other wards for at least a decade. The report told readers that Senator McCarren had the opportunity of his life, and as the father of the second bridge, he would be in line for the election to almost any office he wanted.

In 1893, Patrick McCarren, ignoring the popular outrage against his party, felt total confidence in his re-election. He was running for his third two-year term, and the candidate he had defeated, George Nason, decided not to run a third time against McCarren, who told his lieutenants that they had to find a dummy candidate to run against him to make it appear as if the Republicans opposed his candidacy. McCarren's lieutenants found a bartender named George Owens, and asked him to run against the incumbent. At first, Owens refused because he had no money with which he could mount a campaign. McCarren's aides told him that the senator would even pay his campaign expenses. Owens went to the Republican Committee of Williamsburg for funds to run his campaign, but they laughed at him. They reminded him that he was running against the very popular McCarren, and that he had no chance of winning. Owens grew so angry at the indifference of the Republicans that he tried to resign as their candidate, but he was told it was now too late for him to resign. The overconfident McCarren made some lukewarm campaign speeches, but he felt so assured of his re-election that he campaigned half-heartedly. Owens, however, campaigned his heart out, and made speech after speech attacking McCarren and the Ring.

Election day arrived and everybody, including the Republicans, predicted a McCarren victory. There was revulsion, even amongst Democrats, at the excesses of the ring, and many voted in protest against McCarren, who was its chief legislator in Albany. Many also voted for the straight Republican ticket headed by Governor Levi Morton, who promised to investigate the widespread corruption in Brooklyn.

Exhausted from campaigning, Owens went to bed early, and did not even stay up to hear the election results because he was certain he had lost. Early in the morning, his friends roused him with news of his victory. Owens was angry with them for waking him, and said that he did not enjoy their prank. He told them, "If you fellows had been working like me, you would not think it much of a joke to be roused up at this time of the morning and have a pack of idiots make a guy of you." "Guy nothing," they cried. "This ain't a joke. You're elected you damn fool. Get up you chucklehead. You are the State Senator-elect."

McCarren was shocked at his defeat, and he went into temporary seclusion. He soon recovered from his shocking defeat, and began plotting his re-election. This time he campaigned with all his might and called in all the favors he was owed. His strongest argument for his return to the state senate was that without him, Williamsburg would never have the political clout to build the East River bridge that had been approved, but had been endlessly delayed because of money squabbles.

The Democrats were only temporarily defeated. McCarren was elected again to the senate. He kept his campaign promise by getting a bill for the East River bridge through the senate in 1895, which the governor signed into law. Williamsburg hailed the achievement, and McCarren was feted. The work that began on the seven-year-long construction of the bridge served to remind Williamsburgers of McCarren's power in Albany. In 1900, he also shone in the eyes of the voters when he secured money to condemn several buildings on the border between Williamsburg and Greenpoint to create a park that was first called Greenpoint Park, and would bear his name after his death.

McCarren's support of saloonkeepers, gamblers and even darker elements had become notorious, and was drawing attention, while placing Captain Martin Short and the Williamburg police in hot water. A November 18, 1900, *Brooklyn Daily Eagle* expose informed readers that vice was flourishing in the Eastern District. Readers also learned that gambling houses ran openly day and night and that "disorderly women" thronged the principal streets. The *Eagle* reported:

"Painted and bedizened women, flashily gowned and young women scarcely out of their teens walk the streets and in the sight and hearing of blue coated policemen brazenly accost pedestrians. There is no denying the fact that the police of the Eastern District are fully cognizant of the existent state of affairs, for not only do they countenance the behavior of scores of women who throng the streets after nightfall, but many of the policemen in the district have a bowing and speaking relationship with these women."

The article did not mention McCarren by name, but hinted at his role in supporting vice. The report asked if dive keepers had an understanding with the police, because they seemed free to do whatever they liked. The *Eagle* report mentioned that Captain Short claimed that no power on earth could remove him from his post as long as a certain person in the Eastern District remained his friend, and all the *Eagle's* readers knew that person was Senator McCarren. The article stated that whether Captain Short would be removed remained to be seen. The report highlighting the disregard for the law caused a scandal, and soon Captain Short was transferred out of the district.

1903 would prove to be a crucial year in McCarren's life. For over twenty years, McCarren had been a faithful lieutenant to Hugh McLaughlin, who had grown old and proved unable, or unwilling, to adapt to the new political realities that the merger with Manhattan had created. McLaughlin refused to support the candidates nominated for elected office by their Democratic allies in Tammany Hall, threatening the entire Democratic ticket. McCarren pleaded with his boss to support Tammany's candidates, but the old man remained adamant. Finally, McCarren realized that it was his moment to grasp power. He organized a coup against McLaughlin and became Democratic county leader. Suddenly, he had become the most powerful politician in Brooklyn. Kings County had 34% of all the Democrats in New York State, and the man who now led them wielded huge power.

In December of the same year, the Williamsburg Bridge was opened, and the ceremonies seemed to be a coronation of McCarren's rule over the borough. People recalled the fact that McCarren was the legislative force behind getting his district the longest suspension bridge in the world, and McCarren became the toast of Brooklyn. There was jubilation in the area, especially amongst property owners who knew that the when completed the bridge would dramatically increase the value of their properties. For years, the locals had followed all the stories of its construction in *The Brooklyn Daily Eagle*. They knew every detail of its specifications, as if they had read the blueprints themselves. They observed the building of the span with great anticipation.

Twenty years earlier, the older ones could recall the opening of the Brooklyn Bridge, but this bridge was different. It was their bridge, the brainchild of their very own State Senator, Patrick Henry McCarren. The younger people in the area knew that today would be a celebration they would recall all their lives, and possibly their children and grandchildren would ask them what they did on the day the great bridge was opened. There was an exciting sense that the bridge would dramatically transform the Eastern District of Brooklyn, but they could only guess at all the various changes the new bridge might bring.

If the Brooklyn Bridge was an engineering marvel, then McCarren's Bridge was even more miraculous. It surpassed the first span in many ways. It was longer, wider and heavier. Its towers were higher and stronger, and were made of steel, not masonry. Even the new bridge's cables were far superior. They were far bigger and stronger so that the span could support wider roadways and much more traffic. The new bridge's most superior feature was its capacity. It had two foot-walks, two roadways, two elevated tracks and four surface railway tracks. Tens of thousands of people witnessed the opening ceremonies and the fireworks display in the evening. *The New York Times* spoke of the immense crowds and the cheers of the vast multitude. At one point, a likeness of McCarren's face was even illuminated by hundreds of fireworks mounted on the bridge. When they recognized McCarren's face, thousands of Williamsburgers cheered their hero.

If McCarren had been proclaimed the King of Brooklyn, then there were still those in Manhattan's Tammany Hall who would contest his reign. They believed that the consolidation of 1898 meant that the tiger, a nickname for Tammany Hall, should rule all the five boroughs. The Tammany leader, Charles Murphy, believed that he was the most powerful man in New York Democratic politics, a fact that McCarren should recognize. Murphy believed that now he had the power to rule Brooklyn. Senator McCarren, however, refused to accept Tammany's power in Brooklyn, and organized a resistance under the slogan, "The tiger shall not cross the bridge." Tammany organized a slate of candidates to run in primaries who were committed to destroying McCarren and an independent Brooklyn Democratic Party. McCarren's fate hinged on the results of Tammany's challenge to his authority in the Democratic primaries. Many of the city's newspapers predicted McCarren's destruction at the polls, and to many McCarren's chances seemed dim.

In 1904, candidates supporting McCarren and Brooklyn autonomy won resounding victories over Murphy's slate of candidates. McCarren had emerged victorious, and was proclaimed the King of Brooklyn. In 1905, a Brooklyn newspaper proclaimed that Kings County was almost the personal possession of Senator McCarren.

Chapter Twenty-One:
Ill Gotten Gains

In 1883, Louisine Havemeyer married her aunt's ex-husband Harry Havemeyer in a ceremony in Stamford, Connecticut. The marriage was kept a low-key affair because many of the family were probably outraged not only by the divorce, but also because of the blood relationship of Harry's wives. Lousine made Harry promise that he would give up drinking as a condition of his marriage to her. Unlike her aunt, she knew how to deal with his rages and moments of ill temper. She was twenty-nine years old, and Harry was seven years older. Louisine proved more able to form a loving marriage with Harry than her aunt, and the marriage succeeded.

They both shared a common love of collecting art, although their interests and tastes differed greatly. Harry quickly developed a discriminating eye, especially for three-dimensional objects. His interest in painting developed slowly, thanks to his wife and Mary Cassatt, who had developed a highly refined appreciation for European painting. Under the guidance of Cassatt, the couple would amass one of the largest and most significant collections of artwork in America, and it was soon accurately reported that the Havemeyer home had more great artwork than any American museum.

Louisine Havemeyer would have a war chest of millions of dollars with which she could purchase the finest European art. In its first two years, the Trust made $25,000,000 and within fifteen years of forming the Trust, its profits were $150,000,000 mil. There was also a saying on Wall Street that the stock market gave the Sugar Trust as much profit as the sale of sugar. Few people on earth could rival Lousine Havemeyer's funds to purchase art.

Lousine's union with Harry was fruitful, and within six years they had three children. The couple was determined to build a grand residence for the family that reflected their refined aesthetic tastes, and they would go on to build one of the most beautifully interiorly decorated homes in New York City: a decorative style that was bold, imaginative and, in contrast to many other millionaires, uniquely American. It helped that Lousine chose as her interior designers two of the greatest American interior designers ever: Louis Comfort Tiffany and Harry's old friend Samuel Colman. Together the trio would design a home that was simply stunning and one that redefined American interior design.

The Havemeyers were tired of houses decorated in Louis The Sixteenth style that most of the tycoons lived in. They chose Louis Comfort Tiffany, the thirty-one-year old son of the famous jeweler, who had traveled the world and absorbed many of the decorative styles in the world as their decorator. He was a daring, but ultimately brilliant, choice for a designer. Tiffany's work was dedicated to the harmony of disparate design elements, and melding the varied artifacts and canvases the Havemeyers wanted to display was a great challenge, but one that Tiffany, ultimately, was able to rise to.

By 1889, it was time to build a residence worthy of the mighty family. They hired Charles Haight, who understood that the Havemeyers were self-confident enough to be different. The massiveness and simplicity of their house was different than the residences of their opulent neighbors. It was Romanesque in feel, with rough, cliff-like walls, but the interior of the home would surpass the exterior in its unique difference.

The family moved into part of their house at one East Sixty-Sixth Street in November of 1891, but the interior decoration was still not complete. It took two years, until the spring of 1892, for the interior decorating of Harry's mansion to be complete, but the stunning results were worth the wait. The house was an amazing amalgam of Japanese, Chinese, Moorish, Byzantine, Celtic and Viking elements, skillfully blended into a gleaming, yet harmonious atmosphere for the collection. The entire house was a background for the collection. Tiffany had attended to every detail, and no surface was left untouched. Walls, windows, woodwork, moldings, floors, ceilings and lighting fixtures had all been ingeniously designed. The decorations as well as the hand-carved custom furniture blended perfectly with the soft tones of each room. The interior was completely different than the flamboyant showplaces of many other tycoons who were too unsure of themselves to forsake the styles of the old world.

It was not just the success of the designs, but also their vast variety that aroused admiration. The rooms in the house were decorated with completely different styles, but somehow Tiffany's genius, together with Colman's amazing feel for shades of color, made each room a stunning success. They designed a white mosaic hall with ten pillars at the entrance to their gallery, inspired by the Byzantine chapels of Ravenna. The staircase was an exquisite copy of the one in the Doge's palace in Venice. The walls of the music room were covered with the Chinese embroidery Harry so loved. The library ceiling was a sensation. It was a mosaic of multicolored Japanese silks, outlined with a heavy braid, and the panels were framed with gold moldings. The gallery was not only amazing for its artwork, but also for its flying staircase. A narrow balcony with an alcove ran around the second story of the picture gallery. The staircase, which seemed to hang in the air on its own, was suspended from one side of the balcony to the other. A curved piece of skillfully wrought cast iron formed the spine to which the stairs were attached. The railings were a gold filigree dotted with small crystal spheres. There were amazing Tiffany chandeliers, and the room seemed to be perfectly lit. Visitors gasped in wonder at the glorious interior space Lousine and her designers had created.

Although the interior was stunning, the art was even more amazing. From 1890 to 1892, Harry became adept at hunting up available masterpieces still belonging to European aristocrats. Harry was willing to pay considerable sums for paintings he wanted. In 1890, Harry purchased Rembrandt's *Portrait of a Man*, and what he believed to be a Rembrandt, *The Portrait of an Old Woman* for $50,000. By February of 1892, he owned five Rembrandts in addition to works by Hals. Teniers, and De Hooch. He also had a painting each of Van Dyck, Watteau and Gainsborough. He continued to buy oriental porcelains and pottery, which he was buying for the new Fifth Avenue home. He also collected precious ancient Greek figurines and bronzes.

In June of 1892, a dealer bought him a pair of Rembrandt paintings of a Dutch admiral from a cash strapped princess. He then purchased from the same woman Rembrandt's *Portrait of a Young Man in a Broad-Brimmed Hat*. He now had a room with eight Rembrandts, and his library rightly deserved to be called "the Rembrandt Room." By 1889, he was buying Manets thanks to the help of Cassatt, who soon led them on to buy works of Degas, Cezanne and Monet. Harry and Lousine began to travel to Europe each year to buy art. They fell in love with Spanish art, and also soon became the leading buyers of El Greco and Goya.

The Fifth Avenue residence was only one of the many Havemeyer homes. They owned a "lodge" with three hundred acres on Long Island and a home in Greenwich Connecticut. They also had a "cottage" in Newport, Rhode Island, but the Havemeyers did not enjoy high society in the same way that his brother

Theodore did. Theodore not only had a cottage in Newport, but he was also one of the central figures in the yacht club there. Theodore had a grand residence in Murray Hill, not far from J.P Morgan's amazing estate. Harry's older brother was a sportsman who loved horses and polo, and is credited by many with being the father of American golf. He was the first president of the U.S. Golf Association, and co-founder of the Newport Country Club, host to both the first U.S. Amateur and the first U.S. Open in 1895. To maintain his regal lifestyle, Theodore spent upwards of $30,000 a year at a time when many of his workers made $8.00 a week.

Perhaps the only thing more amazing than the amounts of money Patrick McCarren spent on his love of gambling was the fact that his official salary was just $3.00 a day. McCarren was a silent partner in a construction firm that received many huge contracts thanks to the senator's clout. Reports said that McCarren's annual income was $2,000,000 a year.

In 1908, the failure of the brokerage firm revealed the fact that McCarren was "carrying" $250,000 worth of stock, for which he had paid nothing, and which resulted in a loss to him of about $107,000. No demand had been made by the brokers upon McCarren for margins, in view of this fact he could not have been compelled to pay losses; it was said of him, however, that he gave a check to the receiver and took the stock. He was a "heavy operator" in real estate and in the stock market, and had personal relations with tycoons H. H. Rogers, Anthony N. Brady, William C. Whitney, J. Pierpont Morgan, W. K. Vanderbilt, August Belmont and other Wall Street magnates, of whose interests he was a recognized pusher in the Legislature.

The size of his bets was simply staggering. He was a regular at many New York racetracks, where he gambled staggering sums. *The Ogden Standard* newspaper in a 1917 article said that McCarren was the greatest gambler on horses in New York State history, reporting that he wagered a million dollars a year.

McCarren had a stable of racehorses. *The New York Times* reported that he was the real owner of horses who other people owned in name only, and he wagered huge sums on his horses. However, one day McCarren learned a painful lesson about corruption in horse racing. McCarren staked $75,000 on his horse Ocean Tide to win a race at a Gravesend, Brooklyn track. The other favorite in the field was the horse of the racetrack owner, August Belmont. In the days before cameras, the winner was declared by spotters who were employed by Belmont. The race ended in a neck-and-neck finish amongst three horses, but most in the crowd were sure that McCarren's horse had won by a neck or more. They turned to him to celebrate, but he remained as cold as ice, and told them to wait until the results were posted officially. When the results came, there were howls of protest because Belmont's horse, not Ocean Tide, was declared the winner, and McCarren had lost his $75,000 wager. When Belmont came to shake hands with McCarren the senator was completely poised and gave no hint of his righteous indignation. McCarren soon sold his stake in his racehorses, and learned a bitter lesson about corruption at the track. To remind him of his folly he bought a porcelain walking cane with three horse heads carved at the top of the stick that he carried for the rest of his life.

In 1908, the year before his death, *The New York Times* asked McCarren to comment upon an editorial writer who claimed money was a curse. McCarren said he did not agree with Frank J. Gould, who was quoted in the papers yesterday as saying that money was a curse. But even if it was, he said, he was anxious to find out just exactly what kind of a curse it was. He pleaded with the cartoonists to draw him henceforth as a man who wanted to be a philanthropist, one who took pleasure in handing out money. He had noticed the pleasure it gave other men to hand out money; he wanted so much to taste that pleasure to the full. "I have a great deal before me," he went on. "I now receive a salary of $1,500 a year, and most of that is spent before I receive it."

McCarren was mortified by a bill that was signed into law in 1908, despite his vigorous attempts to block it. The Hart–Agnew Law was an anti-gambling bill passed into law by the Legislature of the State of New York on June 11, 1908. It was an amalgam of bills enacted as Chapter 506 and 507, which were sponsored by right wing Assemblyman Merwin Hart and Republican Senator George B. Agnew. For more than a decade, moral activists, including the Young Men's Christian Association, had demanded New York enact legislation similar to that passed in 1898 by the state of New Jersey, which banned both gambling and horse racing. Newly elected Republican Governor of New York Charles Evans Hughes would advocate changes to gambling laws, and in January 1908 he recommended the repeal of the Percy-Gray Law of 1895, replacing it with strict new anti-gambling legislation that would provide substantial fines and a prison term for those convicted of betting. However, Governor Hughes ensured the law was strictly enforced, and on June 15, 1908 *The New York Times* reported that 150 police officers, plus more than fifty in plain clothes arrived at

McCarren's beloved Gravesend Race Track to uphold the new law. Their instructions were to arrest men who congregated in groups of more than three, plus arrest anyone who was seen writing anything on a newspaper, racing program or even a piece of plain paper, that might be construed as betting.

In 1909, McCarren died at the height of his power. He was just sixty years old. He died because of a punctured artery he had suffered twenty-one years before. He sensed he did not have long to live, and he even bought a suit to be buried in. His one concern on his death bed was the effect that the news of his passing would have on his ninety-seven-year-old mother, who lived in the family home at 97 Berry Street. She swooned when she learned her devoted son was dying, and soon followed him to the grave.

His funeral was held at Saint Vincent's on North Sixth Street. A hundred and ten senators and assemblymen arrived from Albany to attend the service, and a hundred and fifty carriages followed the hearse to Calvary Cemetery where he was buried. As the hearse was pulled through Williamsburg, hundreds of people lined Bedford Avenue to see the great politician one final time. When his will and testament were revealed, people were shocked at how little money he actually had. He had lost a fortune gambling.

Before his passing, he had stated that dying was not very different than losing a bet. His entire career was an improbable bet. Few would have imagined that a self-educated Williamsburg cooper could have become so rich and powerful. Few would have wagered that he could have so successfully aligned himself with the trust and big business for so long. McCarren had lived as a calculating opportunist who bet that he could ride the wave of big business that defined the area during his lifetime. In 1909, the improbable run of luck McCarren had enjoyed finally ended, marking the end of a turbulent era of Williamsburg history.

Chapter Twenty-Two:
Deaths

Sugar brought the Havemeyers wealth and power, but miserable deaths and suicides were the fate of many of the clan, and scandal often accompanied them to the grave. Sudden deaths, divorces and suicides were so common in the family that people began to speak of the taint of the sugar millions.

In 1887, Mary Louise Havemeyer, Harry Havemeyer's first wife, died of a broken heart. She suffered doubly because she not only felt the disgrace of divorce, but also endured the pain of knowing that her own niece had married her spouse. She received a huge amount of money as a divorce settlement from Harry, but she refused to touch any of it. The shame of her situation made her a virtual recluse. She retired to a small house in Stamford, Connecticut, but nothing could assuage her grief, and she died at only forty-eight.

In 1897, Theodore Havemeyer was stricken with a severe case of the flu. Theodore had suffered bouts of bad health, even as a young man. The sickness confined him to his bed in his Madison Avenue mansion, and gave him time to reflect on his life and prepare for death. He seemed to be recovering, but suddenly, he took a turn for the worse, and he realized he was dying. He wanted to make a deathbed conversion and become a Catholic. Theodore, who had married a Catholic and raised his ten children in the faith, converted to Catholicism five hours before his passing. All of the family raced to his deathbed. His brother Harry, fearful of not making it to his brother's side in time, ordered a special private train to bring him down to Manhattan from his estate in Connecticut. He arrived to share the last few hours with his brother. For the first time ever, the refinery was shut down to mark the passing of the man who had built it.

Theodore's passing was commemorated by a high mass celebrated in St. Patrick's Cathedral by his friend of many years, Father Sylvester Malone, and many other priests. The huge bronze cathedral doors were opened as a mark of respect, and as the coffin was carried inside, the organ played the Austrian national anthem. Three thousand people jammed the sanctuary. Father Malone preached a fulsome eulogy for his friend, citing his many acts of charity and his other many virtues.

He left his children shares of the millions of dollars he had earned during his lifetime, but many of them were tainted with the curse of the sugar trust. His son, Carly, who had married one of the most beautiful young women in New York shot himself the following year, just prior to the birth of their third child. Two years later, Theodore's oldest daughter shot herself just like her brother. His wife, haunted by the suicides, returned to Austria, crushed by her children's death.

Father Sylvester Malone's reaching old age seemed like a miracle. Part of the reason why Malone was so loved was his sincere concern for the poor and the sick. He risked his life visiting members of his congregation who were suffering from diseases. In 1878, he contracted smallpox from a sick parishioner, and the disease nearly killed him. He recovered, but would also later contract cholera and ship's fever, both of which severely weakened him. Father Malone finally died on the last day of the year in 1899, a day short of the new century. He had served as pastor for an amazing fifty-five years, and he had seen the total transformation of his church from unwelcomed interloper to rock of the community. Malone died at seventy-eight, and was buried in Calvary Cemetery, his coffin fittingly draped in the stars and stripes. He left a thriving parish with thousands of parishioners, but it was his work outside of the parish with other religions that won him the enduring love of many people in Williamsburg. Former mayors, millionaires and politicians sung his praises, but it was the love of Williamsburg's thousands of poor people that showed what a great man Malone had been. Fittingly, it was a local Jewish woman who was the first contributor to a memorial in Malone's honor.

It was not just people who died, but also, the old city of Brooklyn, which had given a home to the Havemeyer refinery, was also fated to die. Brooklyn was destined to be reduced from the second-largest city in America to a borough in the new city and to lose its mayor and city hall.

The Brooklyn Bridge had physically unified Brooklyn and Manhattan, and bonds of commerce were increasingly joining the two cities. More and more business-minded people advocated for a merger. Advocates of the merger pointed to the financial benefits merging with Manhattan would bring. Brooklyn had its own debt and financial obligations, and a merger with Manhattan would help Brooklyn gain more credit and pay this debt off with an enlarged tax base. Brooklyn, they argued, would share far more tax revenue, and Brooklyn property values would rise. Water was another argument for unification. Brooklyn was badly in need of municipal water, and without water, growth could not continue. Manhattan, however, had constructed the Croton Aqueduct, which offered a huge supply of water to Brooklyn if the two cities merged. There was also an element of pride. Unification would create the largest city in the United States, so Brooklynites could hold their heads up high. In 1890, the New York State Legislature established the Greater New York Commission to explore the possibility of a merger, and in 1894, the question of merger was put to a vote in a referendum.

Many Brooklynites fought unification, seeing in the merger the death of their independence and the demise of the New England style "city of homes and churches." Additionally, they feared that the corrupt Tammany Hall machine would swallow Brooklyn, and infest it with the same level of corruption that plagued Manhattan. No one was a greater advocate for keeping Brooklyn autonomy than State Senator Patrick McCarren, who was one of three Brooklyn state senators who voted against the merger. McCarren said that he hated consolidation, and he vowed he would kill any all measures for consolidation that he could. McCarren feared that bureaucracy would mushroom as a result of the union of the two cities. *The Brooklyn Daily* ran an advertisement for "no" votes before the 1894 referendum that summed up how McCarren and others felt about unification:

> "Every voter can vote 'for' or 'against' the consolidation of Brooklyn with New York. He should vote against it this year, for now is not the time for it. Brooklyn is a City of Homes and Churches. New York is a city of Tammany Hall and Crime government. Rents are twice as cheap in Brooklyn as in New York, and homes are to be bought for a quarterof the money. The price of rule here is barely more than a third of what it is in New York. Government here is by public opinion and for the public interest. If tied to New York, Brooklyn would be a Tammany suburb, to be kicked, looted and bossed as such. Vote against consolidation now and let the speculators wait till a better time, when New York will offer something like fair terms."

The referendum passed with healthy majorities in Manhattan, Staten Island and Queens, but in Brooklyn the merger passed by the razor thin margin of two hundred seventy-seven votes out of 129,211 cast. The bill to unite swept through the legislature, but was vetoed by the mayors of Brooklyn and New York. On April 22, the mayors were overridden, and Governor Morton signed it into law. On January 1, 1898, the independent City of Brooklyn died and the new greater New York was born. For years many anti-merger Brooklynites termed the merger "the great mistake. "

Captain Martin Short died in July of 1904 after a short illness. Literally thousands of people came to his house to pay their respects and thousands attended his funeral. Amongst those in mourning were Patrick McCarren and Jack McAuliffe. He was honored both by the police department, but also by the Grand Army of the Republic of Civil War veterans. Perhaps though the most striking tribute paid to him were dozens of paupers who walked a few miles from Williamsburg to the church at Nostrand and Newkirk Avenues to honor him. They recalled the many times he had reached in his pocket to give them money, and they recalled his many acts of kindness.

One more death would bespeak the curse of the Sugar Trust; however, it was not the death of a family member, but the suicide of a trust victim that would cause outrage. Schemer Adolph Segal concocted a brilliant plan of building a sugar refinery and then blackmailing the Trust to pay him and his investors millions of dollars to shut it down. Segal came up with the idea of building a Philadelphia sugar refinery, but he lacked the cash to realize his scheme. Segal was extremely persuasive, and he convinced millionaire Frank Hipple, President of the Philadelphia Real Estate Trust, to steal money from his investors to finance the scheme. Hipple embezzled $500,000 to build a refinery in 1903. Segal, however, was still short of money, and looked for investors.

John Parsons, the lawyer for the Trust, learned of the scheme, and also discovered that Segal was desperate for cash. Knowing that Segal was so desperate for cash, Parsons arranged for the trust to lend him money, unbeknownst to Segal, who had to put up the refinery as collateral. In a meeting with all the major directors of the Sugar Trust, a plot was hatched to lend money to Segal, but to attach legal strings to the loan that would prevent him from ever opening the competing plant.

Segal did not realize that he was borrowing money from the Trust so clever were they in hiding the real source of the money. Gustav Kissel, the banker who furnished the loan, insisted on Segal's giving the lender an irrevocable proxy over any decisions the directors took, as a condition on borrowing the money. It was Segal's plan to borrow the money, then run the plant, make money and pay it back, but the Trust used their irrevocable proxy to block its ever opening. Segal realized too late that he had been duped. The lenders, who afterwards revealed themselves as the Trust, then pressed Segal for the money, knowing that he was in no position to repay it, while also putting out word that Segal had no means for repayment, killing any hope of other sources of credit. Hipple tried desperately to find another loan, but he could not. In desperation, Hipple committed suicide, and his company went into bankruptcy, while many of his investors lost their life savings.

The Trust was sued in a civil suit, and had to pay $2,000,000 in damages. It also had to return the loan and return $7,000,000 in Philadelphia Real Estate Trust stock that was taken as collateral. The scheme was laid bare in the papers, and the surviving members of the plot were put on trial for conspiracy to restrain trade under the Sherman Anti-Trust Act. Although they were acquitted, the Trust's credibility was dead in the eyes of the public. The criminal nature of the cartel was clear now to all, but there would be even more revelations of the crimes of the Trust that would shock America and send some of its directors to prison.

Chapter Twenty-Three:
Hubris and The Scales of Justice

By 1893, the freight terminal at Palmer's Dock on North Sixth Street and Kent Avenue had grown into one of the three busiest rail yards in the United States, shipping out hundreds of freight cars a day, filled with refined sugar. Thanks to the system of car floats and lighters Palmer had developed, he could sail the Trust's freight cars to any railhead in New York harbor, allowing him to pit one railroad against another in the battle to win contracts to move the tons of refined sugar the American Sugar Manufacturing Company produced. The massive scale of their business allowed the Trust to blackmail the railroads, and Palmer and his red-bearded assistant, Irishman Richard Reilly, could negotiate with the railroads from a position of strength. They knew the railroads were desperate to get their massive business, and would pay dearly for it.

In April 1893, Palmer and Reilly met with New York Central Railroad officials in a secret meeting. Reilly, who had once worked for the New York Central, helped negotiate a secret rebate on all the sugar traffic the Railroad carried for the Trust. The Trust would receive huge amounts of money back from the railroads simply by agreeing to hire their railroad to ship its freight, and no New York railroad could realistically refuse to pay the rebate because it would forfeit a huge amount of scarce westbound traffic. Most of a railroad's business came from eastbound trade, and nearly empty trains often went East, making railroads especially eager to have the massive sugar freight heading west.

Everyone at the meeting knew that although the rebates that they were agreeing to were not yet technically illegal, rebating was an unfair business practice that gave a huge competitive advantage to the trust over other sugar refiners. If news of the rebates leaked out, there would be calls to pass laws to make the rebates illegal, something the Trust wanted to avoid at all costs. Reilly was placed in charge of collecting the rebates, and ensuring that the trust spread its business around so that the railroads all got a percentage of the trade and competed against one another. By 1895, five more desperate railroads were paying the rebates. Reilly would submit bills to the railroads, and when they were paid, he would forward bills to the trust. The rebates totaled to $15,000 a year, just from the New York Central, a huge sum of money in 1894. The rebates were disguised as cartage fees in order to avoid an open violation of the Interstate Commerce Act of 1887, which gave the Federal government the power to regulate the railroads and outlaw such rebates. To further conceal the rebates, the payments were made to the Brooklyn Transportation Company, not to the American Sugar Manufacturing Company. The railroads dutifully paid the rebates for years, even continuing to pay the rebates to the Trust for many years, after such payments were outlawed by the 1903 Elkins Act.

The rebates gave the Trust a huge unfair advantage, allowing the company to quote lower prices in distant markets because it had lower transportation costs than its competitors who did not receive rebates. However, the Trust demanded more than just rebates. Railroads also agreed to provide free storage of sugar at key points across the United States. The free storage let the Trust not only meet the needs of distant wholesalers, but also take advantage of favorable seasonal rates. It could store sugar until the winter, and then sell it when the prices were higher, underselling the competition. Palmer also demanded illegal rebates on his massive traffic in barrel staves, just like the rebates the trust received on sugar. The advantage gained from the rebates meant that no company could produce barrels as cheaply as the Brooklyn Cooperage Company, allowing the Brooklyn Cooperage to set up a virtual monopoly on barrel production.

Although the rebates were illegal, they paled in comparison to law breaking on a far more massive level that was occurring on the docks of the Havemeyer and Elder sugar refinery, just a few hundred yards away. In 1894, the days of duty-free importation of raw sugar ended, and Havemeyer and Elder became responsible for paying a tariff on the millions of tons of raw sugar the firm imported from Cuba, and other sugar-producing countries. An unobservant eye in 1894 would have seen the raw sugar weighed, and government clerks recording the huge amounts of sugar that was arriving at the company docks. A more observant eye, however, would have noticed a cleverly disguised fraud occurring on every raw sugar shipment.

The American Sugar Manufacturing Company employed six clerks charged with weighing the sugar. No government clerks noticed, or at least reported, the crime that was happening right under their very noses. Six massive platform scales that stood in a corner of the docks had been rigged to underweigh the raw sugar arriving in Williamsburg. A mechanical device, attached within reach of the foot of the weigher, permitted a heavy leaden bag to offset the true weight of the sugar so that each scale registered far less weight than the scales actually held. By releasing the wire the scales returned to normal.

Soon, a more efficient, less evident, secret spring was inserted that also under weighed the sugar. Richard Whaley, a company checker from 1892 to 1902, years later testified that he and the other clerks had systematically under weighed sugar for ten years on every arriving ship with the knowledge of the company's dock superintendent. There was even a system of red warning lights to alert those on the dock of the presence of the customs officials. It was customary to reduce the weights by thirty-five or forty pounds on every half-ton of raw sugar. The federal government was cheated out of four thousand dollars of tariff money on every cargo, and the discrepancy between the actual and recorded weights reached some two million pounds of sugar a year on Havemeyer and Elder's docks.

The fraud required an equally dishonest system of bookkeeping with two sets of books. One set of books would show the lower weights that the government registered because of the illegal device. A second set of books recorded the actual weights. The precise company books even had a red ink column to show the difference between the real raw sugar imports and the government weights. No one, however, could see the second set of books without the permission of Havemeyer himself, and for good reason. A careful examination would have revealed that the company refined more white sugar than the amount of raw sugar it imported, clearly an impossibility without the fraud on the docks.

The clerks on the docks had to be bribed into silence. They received extra cash in their pay packets, but they were not the only ones. Soon, some government inspectors themselves were also collecting pay packets at the docks. The government's head weigher was told to see the head cashier, who handed him an envelope each month.

From time to time, evidence of the fraud was revealed, but the bribes and power of the Trust hushed the revelations up. In 1894, evidence of the of the fraud was taken to federal inspector Jacob Kibre, but no action was taken. John Clarkson, chief surveyor for the Port of New York also reported the discrepancies in weights but his reports were pigeon holed. In 1896, an inspector caught a company employee tampering with the scales, but the government took no action, and the inspector was subsequently transferred. The corruption apparently extended to the highest levels of government.

The fraud was not just limited to the scales, but also included chemical tests on the raw and refined sugar. Chemists were instructed to falsely lower results on the tests of the quality of raw sugar that the trust purchased, defrauding the seller out of money he should have received for his high quality raw sugar. After the sugar was refined, chemists also falsified tests so that wholesalers had to pay for a higher quality sugar than that which they had actually purchased. In 1897, William Wakemen, the appraiser of the Port of New York, brought evidence of fraudulent quality tests to the Secretary of the Treasury Lyman Gage who was a personal friend of Harry Havemeyer. Wakemen succeeded in getting two under cover Federal Agents hired, and one of them was paid twenty-five dollars to produce fraudulent test results showing a lower quality of raw sugar than was actually present. Gage said that he could not believe that Havemeyer would be involved in any fraud, and provided him with a letter of introduction to Havemeyer. Wakemen went to Havemeyer and explained to him that he had evidence of fraudulent sugar tests. Havemeyer was very affable, but he became angry when Wakemen asked to see the books. Wakemen realized that he had hit a dead end, and let the matter drop.

Year after year the fraud not only continued, but also even became more sophisticated. In 1904, the Trust started to use a steel corset to defraud the government. A spring was inserted through a hole drilled in the scales' stanchions. If inserted at the right moment its pressure against the walking beam of the scale resulted in creating a false balance. The corsets were fitted into all seventeen of the plant's scales. The scales were placed with the stanchions in dark corners next to the walls so that it was hard to see the deception.

The Havemeyer and Elder plant even defrauded the city on the huge amounts of water it used every day. From 1897 to 1903, the Havemeyer and Elder plant consumed more than five hundred million cubic feet of water. It consumed 2% of Brooklyn's water supply, but the Trust developed another ingenuous system to defraud the city of its water charges. In 1895, the Trust's water fraud started robbing the city of 1,800,000 gallons of water daily. The Trust placed elbow pipes just before the meter that registered the amount of water the plant consumed. The elbow pipes diverted huge amounts of water around the meter and into the plant so that the Trust did not have to pay for these huge water thefts. The water department became suspicious, and placed a meter inside the refinery. The water department quickly noticed the huge difference. They found that the company had also illegally built a private unmetered mane that also drew millions of gallons from the city reservoir. When the city checked the company's books, they found a map showing where the elbow bypass pumps were installed. The city sued in 1909, and they found a man in Los Angeles who had worked for years at the plant. He testified that the bypasses were in constant use during his eleven years of employment at the plant. The damages were reckoned at a minimum of $500,000, but in all probability were much higher.

Harry Havemeyer was not only bent on destroying his competitors in the sugar market, but he was also increasingly turning against the very men who had helped him set up and administer the Sugar Trust. In 1899, he forced out John Searles, one of the trustees of the Sugar Trust out of the seat he held on the Board of Directors. Ironically, Searles was forced out of the Trust for the very same kind of stock speculation Harry himself practiced. Lloyd Palmer who would also soon be forced replaced him on the board out of his position with the Trust.

In 1904, Palmer and Havemeyer had a violent argument over a small piece of woodland that Palmer had purchased in Missouri and Palmer's investment in another cooperage firm. Havemeyer accused Palmer of double-dealing, and of putting his own financial interests above those of the Trust. Palmer subsequently resigned to become President of Squibb Company. Havemeyer approached Palmer's subordinate Richard Reilly trying to discover compromising information on Palmer, but Reilly proved to be loyal to his former employer, and declined to reveal any information to Havemeyer.

Havemayer fired him, but Reilly then formed his own traffic firm, which prospered until Havemayer blacklisted him, and quickly no railroad company would do any business with him for fear of angering Havemeyer. Reilly's business soon withered and one night an officer in the Sugar Trust informed him that Havemeyer had blackballed him. Reilly then decided to cooperate with United States Attorney General Henry Stimson, revealing all he knew about the vast web of corruption in the Trust. Thanks to Reilly's cooperation, in 1904, the government was handed evidence of illegal rebates paid to American Sugar Manufacturing Company by the New York Central Railroad, but Reilly was not done paying back Havemeyer for blackballing him. Reilly not only cooperated with federal investigators, he even accepted a job with the federal government, and Reilly would turn out to be the source of 90% of the federal material sued to prosecute the Sugar Trust.

The Trust had never been more profitable, earning record profits, but Havemeyer was becoming increasingly greedy and paranoid, turning on long-time associates, while refusing to share any of his profits with his suffering workers. In 1906, Havemeyer refused to give the refinery workers an eighteen-cent raise though his company posted a $55,000,000 profit.

A sea change, however, had occurred in Washington with the assassination of President William McKinley. Vice-President Theodore Roosevelt, who replaced him, unlike his predecessor, was ready to vigorously enforce anti-trust legislation and to investigate trust abuses. Roosevelt recalled in his diary how the prosecution of the Sugar Trust occurred.

> It was on the advice of my secretary, William Loeb, Jr., afterward head of the New York Customhouse, that the action was taken, which started the uncovering of the frauds perpetrated by the Sugar Trust and other companies in connection with the im-

porting of sugar. Loeb had from time to time told me that he was sure that there was fraud in connection with the importations by the Sugar Trust through the New York Custom House. Finally, some time toward the end of 1904, he informed me that Richard Parr, a sampler at the New York Appraisers' Stores (whose duties took him almost continually on the docks in connection with the sampling of merchandise), had called on him, and had stated that in his belief the sugar companies were defrauding the Government in the matter of weights, and had stated that if he could be made an investigating officer of the Treasury Department, he was confident that he could show there was wrongdoing. Parr had been a former schoolfellow of Loeb in Albany, and Loeb believed him to be loyal, honest, and efficient. He thereupon laid the matter before me, and advised the appointment of Parr as a special employee of the Treasury Department, for the specific purpose of investigating the alleged sugar frauds. I instructed the Treasury Department accordingly, and was informed that there was no vacancy in the force of special employees, but that Parr would be given the first place that opened up. Early in the spring of 1905 Parr came to Loeb again, and said that he had received additional information about the sugar frauds, and was anxious to begin the investigation. Loeb again discussed the matter with me; and I notified the Treasury Department to appoint Parr immediately. On June 1, 1905, he received his appointment, and was assigned to the port of Boston for the purpose of gaining some experience as an investigating officer. During the month he was transferred to the Maine District, with headquarters at Portland, where he remained until March 1907. During his service in Maine he uncovered extensive wool smuggling frauds. At the conclusion of the wool case, he appealed to Loeb to have him transferred to New York, so that he might undertake the investigation of the sugar under-weighing frauds. I now called the attention of Secretary Cortelyou personally to the matter, so that he would be able to keep a check over any subordinates who might try to interfere with Parr, for the conspiracy was evidently widespread, the wealth of the offenders great, and the corruption in the service far-reaching — while moreover as always happens with "respectable" offenders, there were many good men who sincerely disbelieved in the possibility of corruption on the part of men of such high financial standing. Parr was assigned to New York early in March 1907, and at once began an active investigation of the conditions existing on the sugar docks. This terminated in the discovery of a steel spring in one of the scales of the Havemeyer & Elder docks in Brooklyn, November 20, 1907, which enabled us to uncover what were probably the most colossal frauds ever perpetrated in the Customs Service. From the beginning of his active work in the investigation of the sugar frauds in March, 1907, to March 4, 1909, Parr, from time to time, personally reported to Loeb, at the White House, the progress of his investigations, and Loeb in his turn kept me personally advised. On one occasion there was an attempt made to shunt Parr off the investigation and substitute another agent of the Treasury, who was suspected of having some relations with the sugar companies under investigation; but Parr reported the facts to Loeb, I sent for Secretary Cortelyou, and Secretary Cortelyou promptly took charge of the matter himself, putting Parr back on the investigation.

On November 20, 1907, the government raided the pier based on a tip from a disgruntled former employee. The steamer *Strathyre* with 9,000 pounds of sugar from Java had just docked, and Parr and his crew were ready to catch the thieves red-handed. They inspected the scales and discovered the fraudulent device that underweighed the sugar. At the discovery of the illegal device, Dock Superintendent Oliver Spitzer attempted to bribe Special Agent Parr, saying that the company would pay any amount of money as a bribe if he would just forget that he had ever seen the device. Treasury agents confiscated the device, and arrested Spitzer on a charge of trying to bribe a federal official. The following day, the clerks on the dock were all arrested, as was the company's treasurer Charles Heike, and the refinery supervisor Ernest Gerbracht.

John Parsons issued a statement claiming that the American Sugar Refining Company had just learned about the scales incident. They sent word that they would tender all books and papers pertinent to the investigation. However, when the federal officials came to investigate, many of the most important records were missing. It would take a hundred accountants working six months for the government to calculate the size of the fraud.

There was one man who should have been arrested, but was not: the president of the American Sugar Refining Company Henry O. Havemeyer, who had clearly known about the frauds, and allowed them to be perpetrated for years. Although he was not immediately arrested, he knew that the government was building a strong case against him that would certainly result in his imprisonment. Co-workers and servants had never seen Havemeyer so stressed out and distracted. The idea that he would be imprisoned was clearly weighing heavily on his mind. He could not sleep at night, and he became even more irritable than usual. Havemeyer's family became increasingly worried about his failing health. Havemeyer went out to his favorite country home on Long Island to celebrate Thanksgiving with his family. No one in the family had ever seen him so agitated, and the pall of the government raid on the refinery hung over the family celebration.

After Thanksgiving, Havemeyer and his son went hunting on the three-hundred-acre estate, but soon Havemeyer became violently ill, complaining of indigestion. He was taken home, and a doctor was called for. Havemeyer was bedridden for a few days, and then, on December fourth, his condition took a dramatic turn for the worse. Oxygen was rushed to the ailing magnate, and two other physicians who had been summoned from Manhattan arrived at his bedside, but the patient appeared to be fading quickly. His wife and children joined the doctors at his bedside. He died in the afternoon, and by evening a special train had arrived to take the dead body back to the family home in Manhattan for his funeral. The body was buried in the family plot in Green-Wood cemetery in Brooklyn.

Havemeyer had recently celebrated his sixtieth birthday. His death precluded his prosecution for the massive frauds his firm had committed. Federal investigators determined that the scheme had defrauded the government of over four million dollars, which the trust was forced to restitute to the government. Soon, the men who had done his bidding would have to face punishment for the crimes he directed them to commit.

In November 1909, a new superintendent of the plant was named, and a hundred long time employees of the plant were fired. Sixty-five year-old Ernest Gerbracht and Treasurer Charles Heike, along with the clerks, were put on trial. Gerbracht was defended by former Senator Charles Lexow who had once grilled Havemeyer at a New York State Senate committee investigation of trusts, saying what everyone knew to be the truth: "I would not like to say anything against the memory of the dead, but I am sure that there is not the slightest doubt in the minds here that Henry O. Havemayer knew every detail down to the minutest item. There was nothing about the refinery that he did not know. He had it all at his fingers' end. Gerbracht he ordered around like an office boy." Gerbracht and Heike were convicted, but they had their sentences commuted.

Spitzer was tried for attempted bribery in 1908. He claimed that he had never seen the device attached to the scales until it was presented in court. He was acquitted on the bribery charge, but was convicted on a conspiracy charge, and sentenced to two years in the federal penitentiary. When Spitzer was convicted, he vowed vengeance against the people who had deserted him. He said, "the Sugar Trust made a scapegoat of me. It pounded and ruined me after I had served it faithfully for twenty-nine years." He spent time in prison, but later received a pardon from President Taft.

One abuse remained unpunished: the criminal mistreatment of the workers. The abused men of the sugar refinery would again soon demand humane conditions and fair pay, and again the conflict would cost human lives, and violence once more would erupt on Williamsburg streets.

Epilogue

The Williamsburg Bridge, opened in 1903, and quickly changed the ethic and religious character of the area. Dubbed by some "The Jewish highway," the bridge allowed many Jews to cross over from the Lower East Side and resettle in the neighborhood. The neighborhood rapidly became a vibrant home of Jewish culture. Thanks to the bridge, Williamsburg quickly became densely crowded with even more dilapidated tenements.

Sam Collyer ended his boxing career and returned to the Brooklyn Navy Yard. He also acted on the Vaudeville stage. In 1904, he passed away, and in 1964 he was elected to the Boxing Hall of Fame.

Jack McAuliffe held the world lightweight title for twelve years until his retirement in 1896. He lived for many years after his retirement, and died at age seventy-one in Forest Hills, Queens in 1937. He was inducted into the International Boxing Hall of fame in 1954.

In 1905, Lloyd Palmer left his position with the Trust and bought a controlling interest in the E. P. Squibb Pharmaceutical Company. He also became the Director of the Brooklyn Academy of Music, and heavily contributed to its support. He ran the company until his death in 1915, and left an estate of well over $2,000,000.

After her husband's death in 1907, Louisine Havemeyer focused her attention on the suffrage movement. In 1912, she lent her artistic collection to Knoedler's Gallery in New York to raise money for the cause, and in 1913, she founded the National Woman's Party with the radical suffragist Alice Paul. She was arrested and imprisoned for demanding the right to vote. Louisine Havemeyer became a celebrated suffragist, publishing two articles about her work for the cause in Scribner's Magazine. The first, entitled "The Prison Special: Memories of a Militant", appeared in May 1922, and the other, "The Suffrage Torch: Memories of a Militant" came out in June the same year. Havemeyer died in 1929 and was buried at Green-Wood Cemetery next to her husband. The terms of her will left a few choice paintings to the Metropolitan Museum of Art in New York City. Her final bequest included nearly two thousand works that grace nearly every part of the museum's collections.

In 1910, there was another violent strike at the Havemeyer and Elder refinery, which led to the shooting death of the one of the refinery workers. The workers, however, were still not able to achieve union recognition. In 1917, the refinery burned in a fire, which some suspected was the work of German saboteurs. The refinery was rebuilt and that same year the workers finally were able to unionize. The plant would continue to refine sugar for decades, even after it was sold to another company. Later, the plant became the site of one of New York City's longest labor strikes. The strike started in June 1999, with over two hundred and fifty workers protesting low wages and dangerous working conditions, and lasted for twenty months. Finally, the plant closed in 2004, bringing a long era of local history to an end. The main refinery building received landmark status, but it is to be redesigned as a residence.

Acknowledgments

This book would not have been possible without the help and support of a number of people. I am grateful to my wife Maryla Cobb for her patience and understanding in allowing me to spend the huge amount of time researching and writing the book entailed. I would like to thank Michael Whalen who did a fine job helping me to proofread the text. I would also like to thank Jorge Cruz who was such a perfect combination of talent and patience in formatting the book and helping me to create the wonderful cover. I would also like to pay a debt of gratitude to the librarians at the Brooklyn Historic Society, Brooklyn Public library Williamsburg Branch and at the Schwartzman Library in Manhattan. Great writing cannot happen without great research and these librarians helped me to uncover long forgotten history. I would like to acknowledge Abhay Wadhwa of Gallery AWA for all his backing. I would also like to thank

Acknowledgments

Patrick Gilmour, John Herrick, Joe Doyle, John Ridge, Turlough McConnell, Jenifer Steenshorne, Brant Vogel, Frank Naughton, Professor Maureen Murphy and all the people, too numerous to mention who have supported my writing and research.

Geoffrey Cobb
Greenpoint, Brooklyn
October 16, 2017

CPSIA information can be obtained
at www.ICGtesting.com
Printed in the USA
BVOW08s1258090418
512862BV00010B/40/P